The Future of You:

CREATING YOUR ENDURING BRAND

THE USHEROFF
INSTITUTE, INC.

The Future of You:
CREATING YOUR ENDURING BRAND

By: Roz Usheroff

Published by: The Usheroff Institute, Inc.

Copyright © 2013 Roz Usheroff

Roz Usheroff
2000 South Ocean Boulevard, Suite 102N,
Palm Beach, FL, 33480
roz@usheroff.com
www.usheroff.com

ISBN: 978-0-9896623-0-7

Printed in the USA
First Edition, July 2013

Proofing by: John Firth
Interior layout by: Rod Schulhauser
Cover design by: Jason Machinski
Project Management by: Rod Schulhauser
Marketing Consultation: Jon Hansen

Dedication

In celebration of my biggest champion, mentor and role model, Miriam (Gordon) Gruman, who passed away on June 30, 2012 but guides me in spirit everyday.

Table of Contents

Foreword

By Brian H. Ashe, Past President, Million Dollar Round Table

The Future of You: Creating Your Enduring Brand is a comprehensive, holistic approach to taking charge and managing your career.

The Future of You is an essential guide for all professionals: the senior executive looking to inspire her teams, the experienced employee trying to jumpstart his career, the person who is suddenly "in transition" after layoffs, the entrepreneur building a business, and the recent college graduate.

Have you ever considered what propels some people to thrive more than others in their career? Have you ever wondered why some people get the best opportunities for promotion? Or sought to understand why some entrepreneurs succeed while others struggle or fail? *The Future of You* leads you to create an enduring brand that positions you to succeed in your career regardless of obstacles along the way.

Success is not by chance, but the formula begins with your commitment to grow, explore, challenge, and implement sure-fire strategies. This book is based on the strategies that author Roz Usheroff has taught to corporate executives, middle managers, and employees over the past 20 years. Her message is that to find success and fulfillment you must understand who you are, what your unique value is to your business, and adopt an entrepreneurial mindset of continually marketing yourself and your expertise.

The Future of You dispels the erroneous but widely held belief that security in the business world can be found "externally."

The truth, however, is that in both good economic times and bad, you are your own best asset.

This is critical for every professional who wants not only to survive but to thrive in uncertain business times. By creating your enduring brand—taking charge of your professional plan—you operate from a position of personal strength based on your integrity, authenticity, power, and expertise. As you follow the many strategies outlined in this book, your capacity to thrive will be enhanced.

The Future of You shares a wealth of real-world stories of professional challenges and victories that will both educate and inspire. Throughout the book you will read of the importance of self-promotion—authentically and with confidence. This is not "tooting your own horn" but rather a proactive, positive process to seek out opportunities to showcase your personal best and create a reputation that is sustaining and successful.

Through authentic self-promotion, you move away from an "entitlement attitude" that can be summed up in defeatist self-talk such as "If I do my job I deserve that promotion," or "If I keep my head down and don't make waves I won't get laid off." Instead, you will actively seek ways to demonstrate personal leadership, showcase your enduring brand, and prove your worth.

The Future of You begins with a personal mission statement, then moves into action with a strategy to organize and optimize your assets. You will learn how to discover your "intellectual property" of ideas and talents, develop a networking roadmap, elevate your professionalism, and inspire others as you capitalize on your potential.

In taking charge of your career or business, you will no longer feel victimized by external events or held hostage by office politics. And if circumstances derail your plans or alter your career path, you will have greater access to your own inner resources to find your footing again.

You must become empowered to take charge of your life and your career. With a fuller knowledge of who you are—your values, strengths, and talent—and an appreciation of what you bring to the table, you can devise your plan to create choices that lead to self-fulfillment and success, be it in your career or business.

x

Preface – Are You a Brand to Be Reckoned With?

In a recent *Leader's Edge* newsletter I wrote about the importance of taking a step back and revitalizing your brand. I emphasized the importance of this exercise based on witnessing a rash of situations where people are showing up to work on a Friday and being told that their job is being eliminated within the month. The notable difference when compared to years past is that today no one is immune to the sudden and devastating prospect of losing their job. This includes everyone from the front-line worker to middle managers, right up to the most senior executive.

As a means of protecting your job, I suggested in the article that it was a smart move to take a serious look at the way in which what you stand for fits with your company.

Out of all the responses I received regarding this particular point, one reader's words stood out. Here is what she wrote:

> Thank you for this, Roz. I thoroughly enjoyed reading [the newsletter] and agree with the points you make. Self-branding, aside from company branding, is an area that not enough people do. Some who see the value in it don't know how to go about defining and growing their own brand either.

While this book was already nearing completion with plans to take it through the final editing process before publication, the above comment captured perfectly the core inspiration behind my original decision to write *The Future of You: Creating Your Enduring Brand*.

It speaks to the book's title in that personal or self-branding are areas about which many people do not have a clear understanding. Many still view personal branding as an exercise in self-promotion, which is incorrect.

Self-branding is when you incorporate your values and goals into a clearly recognized image (although I do not think the word *image* goes deep enough) that enables you to leave your indelible mark on the world. Aligning your personal brand with your company's brand means that you will be in sync with your employer's values and goals. It means that you "get it" in terms of where the company wants to go and how you can play a role in both the organization's as well as your own personal success.

What makes me most excited about this book is that it will empower you to realize that everyone has a brand to share and a mark to leave. This recognition is critical given that the corporate landscape is changing rapidly. Instead of viewing your present position as one that is secure in terms of offering long-term employment, you now need to see your work as a temporary assignment. This "transactional engagement" mindset means that you are no longer tied to one employer but instead to those opportunities and requirements that lend themselves to best showcasing and complimenting your talents. This is where personal branding comes into play.

Since the early 90s, I have been one of the most sought-after leadership, image and branding specialists, working internationally with leaders of Fortune 500 companies, executives, managers, sales teams, and entrepreneurs. This book reflects the unique blend of my on-the-ground practical experience with executive suite expertise. It is what has enabled me to successfully transform organizational behavior while empowering both individuals and project teams to navigate the complexity and challenges in the new world of the global marketplace.

In the pages that make up the chapters of *The Future of You: Creating Your Enduring Brand*, I will show you how to identify your personal brand, demonstrate your authenticity, and showcase the best of who you are.

Thanks for coming on the journey,

Roz Usheroff

Introduction – Before We Start, Remember . . . To Thine Own Self Be True

"Our belief does not change reality or truth. You may sincerely believe something to be true, but you may be sincerely wrong."

Like your values and goals, your beliefs are at the heart of what makes you your authentic self.

And just as a portrait reveals the artist's vision, our internal assessment shows the strengths, weaknesses, boldness, and subtlety of our personality. All combined, this creates the canvas from which we carve out our authentic self. Of course, no one trait determines who we are any more than a single brushstroke defines the entire painting. It is in the blending and the contrast on canvas that the intricacy and depth of the portrait is conveyed.

But regardless of your portrait being a work of art to be appreciated, the value is enhanced when it is able to adapt to changing times while still honoring your beliefs.

In essence, beliefs are at the core of our foundation and influence our desire to change or move or try something else. This is a principle that I covered at length in my first book, entitled *Customize Your Career* (2004). Beliefs or "perceptions of self" determine your values and ultimately the goals you both set and work toward achieving in terms of your future success.

It all seems pretty straightforward, yet oftentimes it is not. Somewhere in the hustle and bustle of everyday life, we mistakenly confuse being adaptable to surrendering our own beliefs and values as a means of fitting in.

> If your brand value truly reflects your personal values that align with who you really are, you will have created a magical harmony from within. This in turn will present a unified and sustaining image that will neither disappoint nor surprise, but instead endure.

Instead of attempting to align our authentic selves with our work environment and the job's expectations, we may be pressured to take the route of convenience or least resistance. This is especially true when we are at the mercy of superiors who have their own motives in terms of dictating our actions. In other words, **if you don't know what you stand for, you will be victimized by other people's agendas**.

A few years ago I can remember hearing a story from an individual who joined a personal computer manufacturer as a sales representative. Eager to do a good job and earn commissions, he actively pursued new clients through a variety of activities, including cold calling.

As he started to land new contracts, his sales manager called him into the office for a meeting. Expecting to receive a pat on the back for a job well done, he was instead gently advised to slow it down and, rather than making cold calls, wait for the sales leads to be handed out. "We get so many leads from people and companies contacting us to buy our computers that there is no need to make sales calls. After all," the manager warmly suggested, "you don't want to make the other sales people look bad, do you?"

This is a perfect example of when personal goals may come into conflict with the goals or objectives of the boss or manager. It is at this point that you have to make a decision. Do you sacrifice your own beliefs and values—in essence turn your back on your authentic self—to become part of the herd, or do you remain true to your convictions and the goals that are derived from those beliefs and values?

In the case of the computer sales representative, he had the benefit of being hired by the Vice President of Sales. So, instead of merely falling in line with the edict of his sales manager whose objectives were not aligned with his, he went to the VP and asked if what the sales manager told him was company policy. The VP in no uncertain terms told him that his sales activities are not only expected but very much appreciated.

The next day the VP instituted a new policy whereby sales leads would be distributed according to cold-calling activity. Specifically, the more cold calls a sales representative made, the more sales leads he would receive.

In the end, the sales representative went on to land multi-million-dollar contracts for the company, eventually springboarding him to a senior executive level when the company was purchased by a larger organization.

The above example clearly demonstrates how the person remained true to his authentic self while proactively looking for ways in which he could align his personal goals with those of the company. The challenge was to navigate the complex waters of contradictory objectives with his sales manager.

This is a key point to consider, as you may not have the great advantage of being hired by your boss's boss. There is no doubt that this accessibility through a previously established rapport played a huge part in the sales representative's ability to go over the head of his manager. But even with the benefit of having gone through the hiring process with the VP, there was still a considerable risk with the course of action he chose to take. For example, one cannot help but wonder what would have happened if the VP was not himself committed to his own goals, and instead of rewarding the new sales representative's activities, undermined them by saying nothing and maintaining the status quo—or worse yet, considered the representative's actions to be self-serving and disloyal.

Keeping the above in mind—including the inherent risks associated with stepping out of the reporting hierarchy within your organization—the decision on the part of the representative to do something was nonetheless empowering.

This leads to the question, Are you working to establish connections with those who have either direct or indirect impact on your career and livelihood? Doing so will lead to great empowerment.

Later in this book I will be talking about the importance of networking in both the real and virtual worlds. You will learn why the ability to connect and build rapport with people is even more important today than at any time in the past.

Regardless of the circumstances, one thing is undeniable: Your attitude and actions reflect your values. This means that being true to who you are oftentimes requires you to tap into your internal strength of character. Think of it in the context of being a ship with or without a rudder. When the waters get rough, a rudderless ship—or in this case an individual without a firm set of values, personal vision, and supporting network—will get tossed around, leaving its future vulnerable to the winds of chance. Without a rudder, ships are not in control of their own destiny. It becomes questionable as to whether they'll make it into a safe harbor or run aground and get lost at sea. Conversely, a ruddered ship, while still experiencing the rolls of a violent sea, can stay the course—or at least get back on course having never relinquished control to the external forces of inevitable change.

A Moment of Personal Reflection...

While I was writing this chapter I took the time to think long and hard regarding what values mean to me, and their impact on not only my life but on those with whom I come in contact. As a result of this reflection, I was reminded of the following experience.

Several years ago, I was sitting at O'Hare Airport, waiting to board the plane that would take me to yet another speaking engagement. Lost within my thoughts of going through security, and hoping to make it to the hotel in time to respond to my many e-mails—you know the usual things that occupy your mind when you travel—I barely noticed the beautiful diamond bracelet at my feet. As soon as I bent over to pick it up, I could see that it was an exquisite piece of jewelry. So here I was, at a busy airport, cupping a very expensive item that someone had lost.

What to do?

Turn it in to the guest services counter was the first thought that came to mind. Then I thought, What happens if I turn it in and it isn't claimed? Or worse yet, what if someone gives in to temptation and keeps it?

I called four friends on my cell phone asking what they would do. Each said that I should keep it, providing their reasons for why this was the best course of action. However, my gut kept on telling me that I had to base my ultimate decision on my personal values. So I wrote a note and placed both it and the bracelet in an envelope and handed it to the attendant at the American Airlines counter, informing her of what I had found, and expressing my hope that the rightful owner would reclaim it.

I included the note not for the sake of a possible reward, but to let the owner know that I recognized that such a beautiful piece of jewelry was obviously given as a gift of love, and that I was glad that I was able to have a part in its return.

Several weeks passed before I found myself again in the American Airlines airport lounge.

To my surprise, when I arrived and showed the person at the guest counter my ticket, she paused, then reached behind the counter to retrieve my original envelope. She informed me that the bracelet had not been reclaimed, and that my decision to turn it in in the first place had moved the lounge's staff to the point that they felt I deserved to keep the bracelet.

When I made the decision to turn in the lost bracelet, I never expected to receive a reward, nor did I anticipate that it would be returned to me. That being said, the real moral of the story is not so much my actions—because I felt that what I did was the right thing to do. Nor are the circumstances by which I came to possess something of such beauty the ultimate message that I would like for you to take away from this experience. For me, the real moral of the story was the effect that my actions or value decision had on the lounge's staff.

The fact that the staff were moved by me decision to turn in the bracelet and adamant that I be the final recipient speaks to the true power of our values, which is the impact our values have on others.

What impact are your value decisions having on those with whom you come into contact in your daily life? This is important, because this is an essential part of your personal brand!

A Legacy of Values

Nowhere are the consequences of not being true to yourself and your beliefs more evident as they are in the movie *Wall Street* (1987).

I can remember when I first saw the movie. There is a poignant moment when Charlie Sheen's character—after earning all of his money, winning the beautiful girl, and buying his new condo—is shown staring out the window in the middle of the night asking himself, "Who am I?" It is a powerful point in the film, because after getting all that he had apparently wanted, he still didn't know who he was—or for that matter what he stood for.

To an outsider looking in, Sheen's character had arrived! This young upstart was in the early stages of the apex of his success, with nothing but greatness awaiting him. Of course the character's fatal flaw was that he had knowingly and willingly compromised his personal values to achieve the success that now appeared to imprison him. In the end, the disconnect between his outward actions and his personal values was his ultimate undoing. A very public and embarrassing downfall was the end result.

Saddened by the passing of Whitney Houston, I was again reminded of the above movie scene because I found it difficult to understand how someone with such a special talent, adored the world over, could come to such a tragic end. It would appear that what we saw and who she really was conflicted with each other. I can only imagine how difficult it must be to live up to an outward image that doesn't align with who you really are. In the end, it just doesn't work.

How we align our beliefs with our outward-facing brand—or how we come across to other people—is critically important. After all, in properly aligning these key elements, we determine our living legacy in the here and now.

Create a Living Legacy for Your Future Success

Creating a legacy requires a fundamental shift in the way we think about ourselves in relation to success. This is not about being the fastest rat in the race or being the one who knows how to play the game better than anyone else. This is about acknowledging and honoring who you really are and aligning your goals with the opportunity to feel satisfied with your daily contributions. This also includes aligning your goals with your company's bigger future. After all, when you operate from this dual platform of shared interest and strength, you will not only improve your chances of success, you will also greatly enhance the happiness you experience along the way.

Second, all the success you achieve will mean very little if your beliefs and values are not aligned with your actions, and in turn the enduring perceptions that others have of you. Eventually, and sometimes tragically, this disconnect between the two will come to the surface. When it does, you will be faced with a legacy that, no matter how great your prior accomplishments, will pale beside the revealing light that will show you were not true to yourself.

In the case of Sheen's *Wall Street* character, his moment of truth (or departure from truth) was when he was faced with Gekko's ultimatum to do that which he knew was wrong or walk away. He chose to turn his back on who he really was with the words "Okay, Mr. Gekko, you got me."

Unlike the movies, life rarely provides us with such a moment of transitional clarity.

Never having had the privilege of meeting Whitney Houston, it's hard for me to say when she turned away from who she was and whom she was meant to be, given her amazing gift. However she did turn away. Sadly, and tragically, after she had died, Houston's career and music experienced a renaissance that unfortunately she is not around to enjoy. But the money and the posthumous fame do not make up for the loss to her family and those around the world who were so moved by her incredible voice and presence.

What can we learn from the above examples?

If your actions and outward-facing brand truly reflect your personal beliefs and values, you will have created a magical harmony from within. This in turn will present a unified and sustaining image that will neither disappoint nor surprise, but instead endure. This is the ultimate legacy.

And interestingly enough, this is the first and most important step in your efforts to build an enduring personal and career brand.

So . . . What Are Your Core Values?

It is safe to say that if you ask six different people to define their core values, you will likely get six very different lists. Although there are the general societal mores by which we all must live, there is no one "right" set of values. Or to put it another way, each one of us holds near and dear to our hearts our unique set of values.

So it would appear that the challenge with values is not so much in their existence, but in understanding what they are and how they influence both you and your organization's success.

> The only way you can increase speed and stay on course, is everyone knowing and living the company's values. – John C. Maxwell

Even though Maxwell's statement focuses on the company, it is the values that each employee brings to his/her job that ultimately influence the collective values of the organization as a whole. In this regard, and similar to a chain, the company is only as strong as its weakest link. This is particularly true in an era in which employees are encouraged to think outside of the box and possess an entrepreneurial spirit.

Based on the research of several publications, such as the *Harvard Business Review* and *Forbes*, it appears that the values which are most prized in the business world are the following:

- strong work ethic
- dependability and responsibility
- possessing a positive attitude
- adaptability
- honesty and integrity
- self-motivation
- motivation to grow and learn
- strong self-confidence
- professionalism
- loyalty

After reviewing the above list, ask yourself how your personal values align with the values that are most sought after in the workplace.

How would you define the above values? In other words, when you see the term *honesty and integrity*, what does this mean to you? How would your definition of honesty and integrity differ from that of someone else or your organization?

For example, what if you found a uniquely designed wallet in the street that contained several hundred dollars but did not have anything by which you could identify its rightful owner? Would you keep it? Would you post a notice in the paper indicating that you found a lost wallet and ask the owner to describe it?

What about *loyalty*?

Let's say that you discover that as part of a yet-to-be-announced layoff, some of your co-workers, whom you also consider to be friends, are soon going to be out of a job? Would you keep silent? What if you found out that one of your co-workers was about to purchase a new car based on the belief that his/her job was secure? Would you then say something?

Let's look at *dependability and responsibility*.

You are part of a team at work that must oversee an important company project. One of the members always comes late to meetings and other than the occasional joke rarely participates in any meaningful way. Do you raise your concerns with management? What if this individual is a friend? Would you still say something to management?

Are you beginning to see why and how personal values play such a critical yet complex role in our day-to-day interactions in the workplace?

The examples highlighted in this chapter represent just a few of the possible real-world situations you might face, in which your decision regarding your response may be very difficult.

When faced with challenging situations, I have always believed in Polonius's last piece of advice to his son Laertes in Shakespeare's Hamlet: "To thine own self be true!"

Now Let's Start Building Your Enduring Brand . . .

The following chart provides an outline of my Brand Building Strategy. Starting with your core beliefs, I will take you through the complete brand building cycle. The end result will enable you to firmly align your brand with your organization's goals, while still being true to who you are.

The Brand Building Strategy

What Is the Brand Building Strategy?

The Brand Building Strategy is quite simply an easy-to-follow process that:

- Helps you CLARIFY your core beliefs and how they make you unique
- Points you in the right DIRECTION in terms of aligning who you are with your organization's goals
- Establishes a plan of EXECUTION relative to what you need to do to achieve both your and your organization's goals
- Measures or quantifies the END RESULT of your efforts so as to clearly demonstrate your value to your organization, and in the process builds your enduring brand

Will the Brand Building Strategy Actually Work?

As demonstrated by your decision to buy this book, your willingness to invest your time and energy in self-improvement is clearly evident. That said, you may want to know if there is a guarantee that if you make the investment to both learn and apply the Brand Building Strategy to your career that it will indeed pay off. That is a good question. And it warrants a response of equal merit.

Rather than trumpeting my extensive career as a leadership, image and branding specialist working internationally with leaders of Fortune 500 companies, etc. (which I think I just did), I am going to focus on the true author of your success . . . you!

If there is one single principle or truth that I have learned over the years, it is simply this: You and you alone have the free will to chart your own course for success.

Within this context, my book will serve as your guide as you embark on a very personal journey—a journey that will enable you to identify where you are today in terms of your career or business, and what you have to do to get to where you want to be tomorrow. As is the case with any invaluable guide, I will provide you with the directional framework that will include an A-to-Z roadmap that will take you through critical *true success* checkpoints. These checkpoints will include:

- An assessment of how you see yourself at this moment as compared to how others see you
- Why a personal mission statement is important, and how to create one
- How to establish your memorable brand (including how to identify your unique ability)
- How to be your best PR person

I will then show you how to build a strong support network in both the real and virtual worlds, and how you can best leverage it to your advantage and to the advantage of those you seek to serve. Since being of service to others is also an important checkpoint, I will also help you to personalize the concept of service leadership. Finally, I will help you to create a metric by which you will be able to measure and quantify your tangible success.

In response to the question, will the Brand Building Strategy work, the answer is Yes!—because you will make it work by completing the journey.

Section I—The Brand Building Strategy: Clarity

In the preface to this book I made reference to a response from a reader regarding my newsletter in which I talked about the importance of revitalizing your brand. She said, "Some who see the value in it don't know how to go about defining and growing their own brand." This reader's comment, as is the case in so many areas of life, illustrates how frustratingly wide the expanse can be between knowing where we want to go and knowing how to get there.

In the introduction we took an important first step toward defining and ultimately growing your personal brand. Specifically, we laid the cornerstone of your brand's foundation, which is identifying the importance of being true to who you are.

The next step in identifying and developing your personal brand is to create *clarity*. This includes assessing where you are now in the context of how you see yourself in the world and how it compares to how others see you.

Aligning who you are with the way you are perceived by others is important. After all, it's what others think of you and how they describe you that define your value proposition. **In other words, your brand is the sum of every experience others have had with you.** If there is a disconnect between what you see and what others see, we will identify it, and then I will help you to address it.

Once we have achieved the desired alignment, we will then examine your core values with the intent of creating a personal mission statement. While establishing a personal mission statement may initially sound daunting, it is actually an exercise from which you will derive a great deal of satisfaction. Similar to deciding on a favorite destination for an upcoming vacation, your mission statement will help you to identify where you want to go from a career standpoint, within the framework of your passions and capabilities. You will then be able to align your goals with your employer's or, in the case of being self-employed, your customers' goals.

Or to put it another way, by the end of this first section you will know the direction you want to take and why.

Chapter 1—Audit Analysis: Assessing Past Perceptions and Results

"For want of a nail the shoe was lost."

We are all familiar with quotes such as "Insanity is doing the same thing over and over again but expecting different results." (While Albert Einstein is oftentimes given credit for making this observation, the saying seems to have originated with Rita Mae Brown in her book *Sudden Death*.) And let's not forget about philosopher, essayist, poet, and novelist George Santayana's lament that "Those who cannot remember the past are condemned to repeat it."

Regardless of the saying with which you are most familiar, one thing is certain: You have to have a clear understanding of where you are today, how you got here, and most importantly, what you have to do to get to where you want to go. This is the whole purpose of the Audit Analysis associated with my Brand Building Strategy.

In the introduction I stressed the importance of knowing and being true to who you are. This is how you see you.

The next important steps are to then assess (1) how you are presently perceived by others, and (2) what you need to do on a go-forward basis to set you on the right path to success.

Let's examine the value of knowing others' perceptions.

Assess Past and Present Perceptions

This is a two-fold process. First, you must understand how others perceive you. Whether you like it or not, how others perceive you means that you don't own your brand. Is reality perception or perception reality? Whenever there is a question of who you are, and in the absence of your understanding and input, you allow others to define you based on their own views and preconceived ideas.

An old proverb tells the story of perception...

You define a person's perception by three mirrors:

1. The first mirror is how others perceive you
2. The second mirror is how you see yourself
3. The third mirror is the *truth*

So, what's the truth about you?

As indicated, **you don't own your brand—although you can and should influence its development**. Your stakeholders, or the people with whom you interact on a day-in-day-out basis, own your brand.

Why, you might ask?

It is what others say about you behind closed doors. A combination of your personality, your performance, your values and what you do (or don't do) collectively creates the brand of either your dreams or your nightmares.

Now let's go back to you. The value of knowing how others perceive you enables you to understand why you are getting the results you now have. But you must seek out feedback from different stakeholders in order to understand what people think about you, how consistently you are being perceived, and whether or not you need to modify behavior. Certainly if you want to be a leader you had better be known as a brand that can attract followers. If you are being described inconsistently, or unfavorably, that will inhibit you from capitalizing on your authentic brand.

How to Conduct Market Research

As I was writing this section, several thoughts came to mind. The first was how presidential candidates rely so heavily upon public opinion polls in an effort to measure or quantify their popularity. The second example is how a growing number of corporations are paying significant amounts of money for software that monitors the Internet for any and all references to their brand—be it positive or negative. This is a testimony to the power of the instantaneous and expansive reach of social media and social networking. Within almost a blink of an eye one's image or brand—and with it their fortunes, whether political or business—can change course drastically and unexpectedly. I like to think of this as taking a temperature reading.

Of course from a personal standpoint, your sphere of influence is likely not as wide as those of a politician seeking the highest office, or a major product label looking to gain (or maintain) market share. However, in an age when individuals are encouraged to think of their career in terms of being a start-up business or company, what the above examples demonstrate is that **you have to take an active role in gauging your personal brand's value by understanding how people really see you**.

To start, select approximately ten people (HR, senior executives, colleagues, direct reports and/or customers) to offer you advice on specific areas you could improve upon in order to elevate your presence. Explain that you value their feedback. Make them comfortable by asking what *others* might think rather than asking their own personal opinion. In this way, they will feel more at ease in sharing their true feelings as you are not putting "them" on the spot. Think of it in the same light as if you are seeking feedback for something for yourself but might be too embarrassed to say it is for you. In these scenarios most people will start with "I have this friend who is experiencing this problem…." Asking someone what others think of you is the same thing.

If the feedback is too generic, ask if they can be more specific. For example, "Susan, thanks for sharing that you heard that I can sometimes be impatient. Out of curiosity, would you be able to describe what I do that makes me look or act impatient? This would be so helpful to know."

You have now asked the other person, in a safe environment, if she could provide you with further examples. Whatever comes out of her mouth is how she *experiences you*. This will help you to derive greater value from the research.

One important caveat regarding the above exercise is that you check your ego at the door. In other words, go into the discussion with an open mind. Regardless of what you hear, do not be defensive or attempt to justify your position. Remember, this is how people see you. There is no right or wrong, nor are there good guys or bad guys.

At the other end of the scale, how do you respond if the feedback is all good? In this regard, I can recall the words of one senior executive from IBM who often said, "If we find that we are in complete agreement with each other 100 percent of the time, one of us is redundant."

Now I am not suggesting that you embark on a journey of gratuitous self-criticism. What I am suggesting is that you need to earnestly seek a balanced view, because no matter who we are, we will have undoubtedly rubbed someone the wrong way at some point in time. This is why it is important to seek feedback from ten different people.

> Build greater self-awareness of how others perceive you. Conduct market research and seek feedback from trusted advisors/confidantes/sponsors who will *tell* you the truth.

A True Story

John's story demonstrates the peril of not seeking feedback from those with whom you interact or will be interacting with.

John was promoted a year ago into a leadership role. Defying the need to assess this newly acquired status, John proceeded on his old track of trying to prove his worth, take control, and seek sole recognition for the results. His claim to fame was his one-upmanship. Sadly, he began his new role turning people off and not attracting followers to share his vision of what needed to be done. John never made it in his new role and bitterly resigned.

It's the Real Thing?

Conversely let's consider the number one brand worldwide, Coke, which never sleeps. The bottler expends huge marketing dollars to continuously seek current feedback on customers' perceptions and satisfaction with its products. Coke understands that being number one still dictates an investment in conducting market research to get a temperature reading on what their customers are saying.

Once again, and even though you personally are not a global brand, within your world of impact and influence your brand is no less valuable. Like the old *For Want of a Nail* proverb, which demonstrates how small actions can result in large consequences, it is important to recognize that you are more than just an anonymous, single cog in the scheme of things. You *do* make a difference in the world!

For Want of a Nail

For want of a nail the shoe was lost.
For want of a shoe the horse was lost.
For want of a horse the rider was lost.
For want of a rider the message was lost.
For want of a message the battle was lost.
For want of a battle the kingdom was lost.
And all for the want of a horseshoe nail.

To summarize, in an era in which we as individuals are called to be more than just hard-working employees, you have to first manage perceptions and you must carve out your value proposition. You must conduct market research on how you are perceived by people and why. You must also consistently act in a way that allows others to trust you and to give people permission to give you feedback as your reality check.

This, of course, leads us directly into the second part of the assessment process.

Assess Past Actions

Assess past perceptions of what you did, should have done, and can do moving forward to set up the right path to success. Ralph Waldo Emerson once said, "What you do speaks so loudly that I cannot hear what you say." After spending so much time talking about how you are perceived by others, there is no small irony in the fact that it is your actions as opposed to your words that people will remember most.

Given the importance that is placed on one's actions, there are definite things that need to be done to ensure that you are positioning yourself to build a reputation for your bigger future. Being action-aware, as I will call it, requires that you:

- Know how and why your actions affect others and how this impacts their perception of your value. My true story regarding John demonstrates how the failure to link intent with positive action can be a career killer.
- Step up and stand out! I am not talking about standing on a soapbox and proclaiming to all who listen how great you are. What I am saying is that rather than working behind the scenes, do not be afraid to let other people see what you are doing.
- Recognize that how you are perceived is based on what others know about your accomplishments, not just because you know it. (We'll deal with this in the "Being Specialized" section relating to *strategy*.)
- Be available! Specifically ask yourself if people are seeking you out for your expertise. If they are, continue with what you are doing—only do more of it. If they are not, then become proactive and offer to help others within the framework of your capabilities.

There is another old saying with which we are all familiar that quips, "Those who fail to learn from history are doomed to repeat it!"

No doubt we have all taken one or two missteps in both our business and personal lives. Later in this book I will share with you one of my personal experiences—which by the way still makes me cringe a little to this day. The question is, What if, like John, you missed the mark? Does this mean that you should give up or raise the proverbial white flag? Not at all! However, what is interesting is the fact that it is not necessarily the initial error or stumble that will hurt you the most. It is your response to your shortfall that can cause the greatest problems.

For example, and putting aside the political elements associated with the Kenneth Starr inquiry, President Bill Clinton was not impeached because of his relationship with Monica Lewinsky. He was impeached because he lied about it.

There are of course so many complicating factors that contributed to this particular brand crisis. However I cannot help but wonder what would have happened if, like George Washington and his famous cherry tree legend, President Clinton had told the truth? Or for that matter any President who, when faced with a controversy such as Watergate or the Iran-Contra affair, told it like it is or was.

Washington had the courage to tell the truth to his inquiring father, proclaiming that he "could not tell a lie" and thus admitting that he had cut down the tree. This, according to the legend, ultimately earned the young future President his father's respect. Specifically, George's being honest about the situation more than compensated his parent for the ruined tree.

In reality, very few of us will ever have to face the imposing and likely embarrassing prospects of a highly publicized inquiry when we miss the mark. But the stakes are no less significant when your livelihood is on the line.

In John's case, rather than resigning under a cloud of disappointment and bitterness, there was likely another more productive option. Perhaps John, like Washington with his admission, could have taken that important first step toward rebuilding respect and his brand by admitting that he too had made an error.

The point I am trying to make is that it is never too late to seek feedback from those around you and make the necessary personal adjustments to keep you on the right path.

Key Tips from This Chapter:

1. Clearly identify in your own mind what you believe and what your beliefs represent in terms of who you are and how they influence your outward actions and related goals.
2. Assess how your belief-driven actions have impacted the achievement of your goals.
3. If your belief-driven actions have hindered your success, determine if they are indeed valid or if they need to be changed.
4. If your belief-driven actions are indeed valid— such as in the example of the computer sales representative—determine how you can better align your actions with achieving your goals.
5. Finally, understand how your goals align with those of your organization.

Chapter 2—Creating Your Personal Mission Statement

"Good morning, Mr. Phelps. Your assignment, if you choose to accept it..."

For those of you who have an affinity for classic television from the 1960s, you will immediately recognize the opening line from each segment of the series *Mission Impossible*. Of course for those of you who are a bit younger, the big-screen version starring Tom Cruise will also cause the words "Good morning, Mr. Phelps" to resonate within your collective memories . . . at least with the first movie anyway.

Regardless of the era, the one common thread that runs through this invitation to a challenging mission of adventure and excitement are the words "if you chose to accept."

In many ways, creating your personal mission statement based on the values associated with your beliefs and how they align with outside perceptions is indeed a challenge to be embraced! Drafting a tangible action plan in writing will reinforce your commitment and steadfast focus. Think of it as a contract with yourself that should not and cannot be broken. After all, if you can't make and keep a promise to yourself, how will you be able to do so with others—including your company or client?

So What Is a Personal Mission Statement?

Paul B. Thornton, who is a professor of business administration as well as the author of twelve books including *The Answers Are on the Office Wall*, once said, "Without mission, there's no purpose. Without vision, there's no destination. Without values, there are no guiding principles." A personal mission statement provides clarity and gives you a sense of purpose. It defines who you are and how you will live.

Although the above statement starts off by emphasizing the importance of having a life's mission, I personally believe that the words of Napoleon Hill are more beneficial when one is seeking to identify life's purpose. In Hill's seminal book *Think and Grow Rich* (2009), he presented the idea of a Definite Major Purpose as a challenge to his readers in order to make them ask themselves, "In what do 'I' truly believe?" Hill went on to observe that 98 percent of all people have either few or no firm beliefs. This alone, according to the American author, puts true success firmly out of reach.

Hill's perspective is one of the reasons why, in the introduction of this book, I chose to focus on the importance of knowing your personal belief system. Before you can even contemplate the outline for a personal mission statement, you must either confirm and/or establish your belief system and core values. Once you have completed this critical first task, you will then be ready to create your life's blueprint.

Of course when I first began championing the importance of developing your own mission statement it was considered outside-of-the-box thinking, in that such an exercise was usually conducted within the framework of a corporate entity. Back then, the thought of creating an individual roadmap to success was the antithesis of building and being part of a corporate team.

Besides being viewed as a self-serving activity, efforts to stand out from the crowd were often met with hostility and disdain from fellow employees. (Remember the story of the computer sales representative?)

Today, and with books such as *The Start-up of You: Adapt to the Future, Invest in Yourself, and Transform Your Career* (Hoffman and Casnocha, 2012) serving as a personal call to action, it has become clear that the rules of the game have changed dramatically. Instead of being a selfish or self-serving act, the failure to draft your own mission statement is now considered to be irresponsible in that, like our rudderless ship analogy in the introduction, you have no means by which you can navigate the shifting tides of inevitable change.

The Key Elements of a Personal Mission Statement

I remember giving an interview a few years back during which I was asked to explain the foundations of a personal mission statement. As indicated earlier, it was an interesting question, because at that time very few people actually had one. I began by saying that a key part of a personal mission statement is that it enables you to identify or come to know your unique talents and expertise, as well as the gifts you bring to the table. In promoting your mission statement, you need to view it through the lens of how your skill sets can then be used to benefit other people. This is an important part of the process, as we know that by helping other people to succeed, you in turn will also experience success.

In this way, a personal mission statement is actually a selfless act. Instead of being a self-serving game plan, it is in effect a means by which you can identify ways to use your unique abilities to help others and the organization for which you work.

Or to put it another way, **by using your personal mission statement as a vehicle through which you can help others, you actually become a part of a much larger collaborative community**. In your case, the community could be those individuals within your organization or your customers.

As you begin to contribute to this "collective" success by aligning your objectives with those of the organization, you will be better positioned to realize your own aspirations or personal goals. However, getting there has to extend beyond a mere conceptual sentiment. There has to be a definite plan of action or strategy put into place that will enable you to create the success that you seek. This means that your mission statement has to be based upon a clear-cut vision that is centered on your beliefs and values. A vision that, when aligned with your organization's objectives, becomes your path to success.

> The mission statement helps you to identify and articulate your beliefs and core values. This highly personalized statement becomes your motivation and the gauge by which you measure your actions, plans, and strategies for the future.

Tips on Crafting a Personal Mission Statement: Who, What, and How

What unique gifts and talents do you have? How do you want to use them and for what purposes? These are the key elements of your personal mission statement.

Consider these three words to help draft your own mission statement: *who*, *what*, and *how*.

Who? Describe yourself. What talents, gifts, and attributes do you bring to the business world?

What? Outline your goals for the use of those talents, gifts, and attributes.

How? Describe the outcome, including the impact that you want to make and the impression that you want to leave behind. How will you make a difference?

Your personal mission statement might look something like this:

"My personal mission statement is to use my leadership and communication skills to help others increase their personal power and elevate their unique talents in the corporate world."

"My personal mission statement is to share my wisdom and direction with the highest level of integrity to help people achieve their dreams."

"My personal mission statement is to offer creative solutions to my team and customers where our value is seen and appreciated."

A Final Thought . . .

Choose your goals wisely, as they will influence your core values—and ultimately how you write your mission statement. If your goals are based on self-serving gain, you may find that your values do not support your mission. As you will discover from the experiences of famed Canadian musician and record producer David Foster, this kind of disconnect usually leads to failure.

Foster, of course, discovered singers such as Michael Bublé and produced major stars such as Mariah Carey, Céline Dion,

Madonna, and Michael Jackson. When he was asked about his accomplishments, he had this to say: "Whenever I embarked on a project in which I was focused on making money, I inevitably failed." The key, he would add, is to pursue your passion and do those things that are not based on getting rich, but that serve your craft as well as others.

To me this says it all, because it is the cornerstone of an effective personal mission statement.

Key Tips from This Chapter:

1. Identify the talent, expertise, and the unique gifts you possess.
2. Beyond promoting yourself, understand how your mission statement will help others and/or make a difference in the lives of those with whom you come into contact.
3. Develop a clearly outlined strategy to create the success that you seek through your mission statement.
4. Be true to yourself by basing your decisions on the values associated with your mission statement.
5. Finally, have confidence in both yourself and your personal mission statement, as it is your career and life plan.

Section II—The Brand Building Strategy: Direction

Now that you have identified your core values and clarified your capabilities—as well as brand value—through the creation of your personal mission statement, it is now time to chart a tangible course for your ultimate success. What I am talking about is establishing an indelible brand that will place you and keep you in high demand.

Note that I did not say "create job security relative to your present position." As indicated previously, the notion of job security is a faint memory of a bygone era. Establishing an indelible brand that will keep you and your capabilities in high demand has very little to do with a sole, long-term employer.

In today's global marketplace, the ability to adapt to different situations and requirements—oftentimes with different companies—is the key to your ongoing success. This doesn't necessarily mean that you won't spend any number of years with the same company. This can and still does happen. What it does mean is that you cannot depend on it.

With alarming frequency we are beginning to see that *no* one— and I mean no one—is immune to the possibility of waking up one morning to find that he/she is out of a job. This even goes for those who have inhabited the lofty heights of the executive suite.

Imagine, for example, that you are a senior director within a major corporation. Imagine that for the last three years you have been groomed for a VP role with global client responsibilities. Imagine that you are now promoted, with cool perks like business-class travel and a membership at a prestigious golf club to enjoy with customers. Or a designated limo at your disposal to whisk you off to meetings, corporate events, etc. Fast forward three months into the position and your boss, who was your biggest champion and mentor, leaves unexpectedly. Headhunters are now scouring for his replacement. NOW imagine . . . what will happen to your role when the restructuring starts to happen? How solid is your brand position?

Does this sound like an extraordinary, perhaps even impossible, turn of events? Even though it seems unbelievable, it is indeed a true story!

What the above example illustrates is that you are being naïve and vulnerable if you believe you are irreplaceable. You must always have a contingency plan or you will allow others to control your career direction. You must know the value of your brand, which will put you at a definite advantage if your present situation changes suddenly.

In short, in the words of the Boy Scouts, it pays to be prepared.

The next few chapters will help you to BE PREPARED.

Nothing Is Forever: A Cautionary Tale

There are many stories about individuals whose careers suddenly took an unexpected turn, catapulting them into uncertainty from a seemingly comfortable and secure position. One that immediately comes to mind for me is that of a close friend's husband. The husband worked for a prestigious furniture company in Montreal, Canada. Based on his performance in Montreal, and wanting him to achieve similar success in the main office, his boss made the decision to move him and his family to Toronto. A year later, the boss who had brought the man and his family to Toronto was suddenly fired.

Unfortunately, my friend's husband did not have a contingency plan. Why would he? After all, wasn't he a proven performer who was moved to Toronto to grow the business? Yet he was nonetheless vulnerable because he never branded himself nor created a value for his services beyond the need he filled for his now departed boss. Outside of a narrow circle of contacts he was relatively unknown. Did he really think that his boss was forever? He made this assumption forgetting that nothing is guaranteed.

In the upcoming chapter of this book I talk about the importance of being memorable. What the above story cautions is that *who* remembers you (or is still around to remember you) is of equal if not greater importance.

Chapter 3—Be Memorable

"So the last thing I want to say is, when I was young, there was this section in the Reader's Digest. And it was called "The Most Unforgettable Character I've Ever Met." And for me that person is Sonny Bono. And no matter how long I live or who I meet in my life, that person will always be 'Son' for me."

In what was undoubtedly one of the most moving eulogies ever delivered, Cher's final words regarding Sonny Bono stand out for their heartfelt sincerity. Despite the tumultuous life events that had led to many conflicts and ultimately the dissolution of their marriage, the fact that Cher would, with such fondness, refer to Sonny as "the most unforgettable character I've ever met," speaks to the very essence of this chapter.

While it is clear that Sonny Bono was cherished by Cher, I could not help but wonder what makes someone unforgettable. Or in the context of this book, what makes them memorable?

Dr. Nido Qubein, who wrote the introduction to my book *Customize Your Career*, said: "If you want to have success and significance—in business and in life—choose to be a person of value!" Qubein, who is a business leader, Chairman of Great Harvest Bread Company, President of High Point University since 2005, as well as being on the board for companies such as La-Z-Boy and BB&T, equates value with personal power.

Perhaps **being a person of value is the secret element to becoming a memorable personality**. But is it really such a secret? As we have already discussed in the previous chapters, we are indeed living in a dramatically changing world where every opportunity to demonstrate your value is critical to your ongoing success.

In the Audit Analysis in Chapter 1, in which you assess past perceptions and results, I challenged you to ask yourself: **What is it that I do that adds remarkable, measurable, distinguished, and distinctive value to the lives of others?** In other words, you have to **think in terms of the experience and outcome you create for others**.

Of course how you serve the best interest of others can take many forms. This can even include dealing with a difficult, perhaps even uncomfortable, situation head-on. (Remember my references to Bill Clinton and the George Washington legend?)

As already covered in the previous chapters, your brand begins to take shape when you understand your values and those things that matter to you the most. You then verbalize these values in the form of creating a personal mission statement. This is your brand's foundation, and it becomes the rudder to help you successfully navigate your ship through difficult waters—to arrive safely at your chosen port of calling.

The Tylenol Crisis

I can think of no better example to demonstrate the important link between one's value-oriented mission statement and building a memorable brand than the 1982 Tylenol tampering tragedy.

For those of you who may be too young to remember, Johnson & Johnson recalled 31 million bottles of its flagship brand, Tylenol, after it was reported that seven people in Chicago had died due to product tampering. An unknown suspect had put 65 milligrams of deadly cyanide into Tylenol capsules. The tampering occurred at the retail level, and in this regard, Johnson & Johnson was as much a victim of the crime as were those who tragically lost their lives.

Even though the recall produced a loss of more than 100 million dollars and a drop from a 37 percent market share to 7 percent, the company's willingness to place the interests and safety of its customers ahead of its own was clearly demonstrated by: (1) a quick acknowledgment of the problem, (2) the implementation of a decisive and effective response, and (3) open and ongoing transparent communication with the public.

These monumental decisions at a critical point in the company's history were based on the Johnson & Johnson Credo (mission statement), specifically the emphasis on protecting people first and property second. Written in the mid-1940s by Robert Wood Johnson, the Credo represents the "values that guide" the company's decision-making process. One could reasonably argue that without the existence of the Credo, decisions surrounding the tampering crisis may have been different.

Think about it for a moment. The Johnson & Johnson document created in the 1940s was the basis upon which the company responded to a major challenge in the 1980s. Over a 40-year period the Credo's values were ingrained into the company and, like a ship's rudder, were relied upon to take the company through one of its most difficult periods ever. In other words, the fast decisions that the situation demanded were based on known and entrenched values as opposed to being a "strategic" reaction developed on the fly. Or to put it another way, the response was second nature.

Following the crisis, when the Tylenol product was re-launched, Johnson & Johnson once again based their decisions on their Credo. This meant that the company took significant measures to deter tampering. These measures included the introduction of a caplet, and triple-seal tamper-resistant packaging. Johnson & Johnson's 2,250 sales people also embarked on a major campaign to win back the confidence of the medical community through a series of presentations.

Today, the company has restored its brand as the most trusted over-the-counter pain reliever, outselling the next four leading painkillers combined, including Anacin, Bayer, Bufferin, and Excedrin. Suffice it to say, both Johnson & Johnson and its Tylenol brand are trusted and memorable.

However, knowing your value and demonstrating it are two very different things.

> Consider every opportunity as a chance to improve and promote your bullet-proof brand, as well as make it memorable for all the right reasons. Don't delegate this responsibility to other managers—take the lead in every situation. Life is not a dress rehearsal!

From a personal standpoint, it begins by honoring not just your values, but those of your partners. Honor them for their differences and treat them with respect.

It's about building your reputation while presenting a consistent (and memorable) brand that is represented in your mission statement and aligned with the best interests of your internal and external customers.

It's about knowing the basic rules in different settings: how to conduct yourself in meetings, business and social settings, how to build rapport, and how to use appropriate behavior at all times. It's about standing out and fitting in simultaneously.

Unfortunately these principles are not always demonstrated when needed.

As memorable as the Johnson & Johnson response to the Tylenol tampering crisis was in terms of overall effectiveness, Exxon's poor reaction to the Valdez oil tanker spill is equally memorable . . . for all of the wrong reasons!

The *Exxon Valdez* . . . A Rudderless Ship

While Johnson & Johnson was not responsible for the problems relating to product tampering, the company still took ownership of the situation and moved quickly to formulate a response based on its longstanding Credo. As previously stated, they quickly acknowledged the problem, took immediate action to address it, and, from start to finish, maintained open communication with the world.

Exxon, conversely, was, for the most part, responsible for what happened when its oil tanker, *Exxon Valdez*, ran aground, causing 32,000,000 US gallons of oil to empty into Prince William Sound in Alaska. When faced with this monumental crisis, the press was initially met with a "no comment" by company officials. From that point on, Exxon's leadership became evasively defensive, ultimately never taking ownership for their role in what had happened.

While Johnson & Johnson was able to restore confidence in its brand, Exxon's failures sent out the message that the company did not care about the environment, or how it damaged the Alaskan economy. Like the approximate 26,000 US gallons of *Valdez* crude oil still in Alaska's sand and soil, the company's brand remains tarnished to this day.

When Will They Ever Learn?

Unfortunately, and in line with the axiom, those who fail to learn from history are doomed to repeat it. Fast forward to 2010.

When British Petroleum's CEO Tony Hayward apologized to the Gulf Coast residents for the worst oil spill in US history, he shamelessly commented on the toll that the spill was taking on "his life"! In fact, he was quoted as saying, "I'd like my life back."

Going beyond my difficulty with contemplating the sheer magnitude of the Gulf Coast spill in contrast to the enormous amount of crude oil that was dumped by the Exxon Valdez, one cannot help but wonder, *What was Hayward thinking?* Here we are dealing with what the US Department of Justice referred to as being "an act of gross negligence" on the part of BP, and the CEO of the company is holding a pity party saying that he just wants his life back. Sadly, rather than focusing his attention on the best interests of those upon whom his company's actions had a negative effect, he chose to publicly whine about his own situation.

Within the context of these contrasts, there are definitive steps you must take to stand out and be remembered for all of the right reasons.

Becoming Memorable

I recently had the privilege of speaking at a major pharmaceutical conference where I facilitated my Dare to Be Remarkable interactive workshop.

As I had alluded to in the opening paragraphs of this chapter, someone memorable is worth noticing. Someone memorable is worth talking about and is seen as being exceptional. Someone memorable stands out and is recognized for his/her value, trustworthiness, unique abilities, and personality.

Here are the top seven strategies for moving from ordinary to extraordinary.

1. Be Remarkable

Beyond the obvious and what we have already covered, I would just like to share some thoughts of Seth Godin, author of *Purple Cow: Transform Your Business by Being Remarkable* (2009). Godin believes that in order to be remarkable, you must have a Purple Cow. That is, something that enables you to stand out from the crowd.

Of course, once you have created your Purple Cow, there are two things that are critical to remember. To start with, you have to diligently "milk" the cow for everything it's worth. This means you have to figure out how to profit from what makes you remarkable for as long as possible in a "make hay while the sun is shining" sort of way. While you are focused on maximizing the benefits of your current Purple Cow, you also have to keep an eye to the future. Specifically, you need to know when and how to reinvent your Purple Cow in enough time to replace the old one when its benefits inevitably wane.

There are many examples of individuals who have successfully reinvented themselves, or successfully created a new Purple Cow. In one of the more pronounced transformations, Dwayne "The Rock" Johnson left behind his professional wrestling persona to become a major film star, appearing in movies such as *The Scorpion King*, *Get Smart*, and *Race to Witch Mountain*.

Madonna is a testimony to staying power by reinventing her brand multiple times spanning several decades, as did Joan Rivers, whose turn on *The Celebrity Apprentice* once again catapulted her into America's living rooms. She went from being a stand-up comic and talk show host to developing and promoting her own line of jewelry to competing and winning on Trump's *Apprentice*.

But to me no one exemplifies the ability to perpetually reinvent themselves better than Betty White. Reflecting back on her career that has spanned nine separate decades, White has been masterful at playing to her strengths and age in hit shows such as *The Mary Tyler Moore Show*, *The Golden Girls* and most recently *Hot in Cleveland*. She has even defiantly (and humorously) heralded her golden years in her latest television project as the host of the practical-joke show *Betty White's Off Their Rockers*. Talk about an enduring personal brand!

While there are many more examples to which I could refer, the key is that all of the above individuals recognized that their current brand had a shelf life and, in acknowledging this reality, they were willing to take risks and try new things.

I am certain that each of these individuals went through their own process of honest self-evaluation, which probably included their seeking feedback from trusted confidants (as recommended in Chapter 1).

Of course what you decide to do with this feedback is entirely up to you. However, when seeking the advice of others, be careful not to look for reassurances about what you are already doing. To be truly beneficial, you should not only want but also welcome honest criticism from your objective sources.

As you will note with each of the individuals to whom I have referred, they demonstrated a willingness to change and ultimately to adapt to a new reality. **This is the key to being remarkable: Focusing not on what you are doing now, but what you have to do differently to step-up and stand-out**.

So how do you stand out? What's remarkable about you that prompts others to talk about you? Remember, you have to be worthy of being talked about, which may mean that you have to get back to the drawing board and create your own distinct and indelible mark!

To help you with this task, here is an exercise you can do that will enable you to discover and capitalize on your own memorable brand.

Exercise:

- Identify three achievements that you are most proud of. What skill sets did you use to create these accomplishments?
- Identify ways in which you presently differentiate yourself from others. What strategies have you found to stand out?
- Identify how you create a lasting impression. What makes you stand out and be remembered?

With your answers to the above questions, you will have established the outline for designing your unique differentiating attributes.

Keeping in mind that your brand is "the sum of every experience others have of you," you now have to ask yourself how these attributes have: (1) caused you to be noticed, (2) made people remember you, (3) motivated them to seek out your advice, and (4) created trust.

Based on the extent to which you have impacted the lives of others, you will then be able to focus your energies on doing more of what makes you stand out and become visible.

This nicely segues into our second strategy.

2. Be Visible

As a brand, which is how you build your reputation, you have two stages from which to operate: front stage or back stage. Front stage positioning means that you make it your business to be visible and heard, while back stage positioning simply means that you do your magical work from behind closed doors.

What is interesting about the front stage/back stage positions is that the perceptions of both are usually and universally misunderstood. For example, we have all encountered the individual in a meeting who refuses to shut up, even though she knows that she is dominating the conversation. While others in the meeting consider her actions to be tantamount to hogging the spotlight (i.e., taking front stage), she is ironically seen by upper management as being a team player and engaged. At least she is participating!

Conversely, those who blend into the background (i.e., place themselves back stage) view themselves as being thoughtful and humble in that they cede the floor of discussion to others. They believe that unless they have something special to contribute, they are better off taking a back stage position.

However, by remaining silent and believing that their results will speak for them, the quiet individuals are oftentimes mistakenly viewed by upper management as being disengaged, distracted, or not confident.

You might now be asking yourself the question, "Why is there this disconnect between what we have been conditioned to believe and reality?" Specifically, is it really true that, like the axiom about the squeaky wheel getting the oil, those who are front and center at meetings and throughout the day are the ones getting ahead?

The truth is that with a more vocal contribution, you assume a front stage position that puts you in the limelight. This in turn forces you to be a contributor, to be heard, and to take risks. It makes you face the truths about what's happening outside of your world. Yes, it can produce tremendous amounts of stress, but it is more likely a positive, energizing kind of stress compared to back stage anonymity.

Conversely, some people try to stay under the radar screen in the workplace and not attract attention. I call this back stage sabotage. Even though they believe that it's a safer stage upon which to play, I have found that people who remain in the background suffer a high degree of uneasiness as they are always looking for someone to both notice and acknowledge their efforts. This kind of strategy is more often than not a futile and self-defeating proposition, as they are leaving it up to someone other than themselves to define their brand.

In other words, while you feel sheltered from the risks associated with office politics and the increased expectations of being seen, you're also not being recognized for what you bring to the table. This latter position leaves you more vulnerable to being passed over for a promotion or, worse yet, seen as someone who lacks a genuine interest in the job and the company.

A Moment of Personal Reflection...

. . . It is as though I have been surrounded by mirrors of hard, distorting glass. When they approach me they see only my surroundings, themselves, or figments of their imagination— indeed, everything and anything except me.

The above excerpt from the famous Ralph Ellison novel *Invisible Man* is telling in so many ways relative to our visibility at work and even sometimes in life. This is due to the fact that in the hustle and bustle of meeting deadlines, interacting with customers, and responding to changing business realities, we oftentimes get lost in the shuffle.

However I believe that the issue with anonymity goes well beyond the contemplation as to whether or not we are seen and noticed to one of personal responsibility. Specifically, if you are not being seen and not being heard, then you have to take ownership for your absence of presence!

Visibility, as I have always said, is not based on perfect attendance. You cannot simply show up and do a great job.

Take the example of a promising executive, Janet, who was asked to temporarily replace her boss while he was absent for a month. Although shining in her role as his temporary replacement, ironically she wasn't considered a viable candidate to fill her boss's position on a permanent basis when he was later promoted. Janet was devastated that, instead, a male counterpart was given the promotion. Hadn't she been the one selected to fill in during the former boss's absence? Hadn't she done an excellent job during her effective albeit brief tenure in the top spot?

With these questions running through her mind, Janet approached her now former boss to ask him why she had been overlooked. His response should be a sobering reminder of the importance of having a visible and memorable presence.

To begin with, he expressed surprise at her disappointment for not getting the promotion, as he did not even know that she was interested in the position. In fact, he explained that his new replacement had expressed on several occasions in the past year that he wanted to be promoted. But Janet, like so many, believed that her work should speak for itself. As this story illustrates, if you don't express your needs and share your career aspirations, you fall into the trap of becoming unnoticed, much like Ralph Ellison's Invisible Man.

The above comments provide a powerful lesson that, no matter how well you do your job, toiling away in obscurity will inevitably cause you to miss opportunities for which you might otherwise have been ideally suited. Add into the equation today's tough economic climate and you might also find yourself out of a job.

So what should this executive have done to place herself in a position to be promoted?

Quite frankly, as soon as she assumed the helm of leadership during her boss's absence, she should have used it as an opportunity to network with senior management. After all, filling the boss's shoes, so to speak, represented the perfect reason for breaking the ice and building both a rapport and presence with the very individuals upon whom her future career was dependent. In conjunction with doing an excellent job, her increased interaction with senior leadership would have created a higher level of comfort with and confidence in her as a prospective "new" boss.

The moral of this story is pretty simple. To move from the ranks of the invisible, you have to become your own publicist and reach out to a larger circle of people.

Like the Sun Tzu axiom that contends that most battles *are won or lost long before the fighting begins*, you will, by creating visibility, position yourself to strike while the iron is hot and emerge the victor!

Janet's story reinforces the fact that you must take responsibility for your future. If you go unnoticed, as witnessed here, other people will make decisions for you.

Janet should have been proactive and discussed her desire to be promoted to her boss's position before she was given the temporary reins in his absence. As already stressed, sharing your vision and aspirations are essential for demonstrating that you have ambition and drive and purpose. It is also the reason why it is important that your goals align with those of the company. This is why a personal mission statement is so important.

While some bosses may feel threatened by this approach, this can easily be avoided if you tell your boss that you want to partner with him, support him in his work, and make it clear that you are committed to helping him succeed. When you make your boss the hero in your story, you will naturally create a win-win situation. This in turn paves the way for you to: (1) share your dreams and aspirations with your boss, (2) engage with senior management, and (3) identify those opportunities through which you can best showcase your capabilities.

Had Janet had the courage to be honest with her boss regarding her personal goals, used her position during his absence to build rapport with other members of the senior management team, and then performed as she did, the outcome would have likely been different.

So what can you do to avoid making the same mistakes as Janet?

The following exercises should help.

Exercise 1: Building Your "Fan Base"

- Make a list of those individuals who you can call upon to support your ideas, initiatives, and suggestions in future meetings.
- Make another list of those individuals who have relationships with decision makers with whom you do not have direct access but would be willing to speak on your behalf to introduce or reiterate your suggestions.
- Now, identify two tactics that would help you to demonstrate your appreciation and reciprocate appropriately.

1. _____

   _____

2. _____

   _____

Remember, your brand is the sum of every experience others have of you.

To stand out, you have to creatively highlight what makes you different, better, wiser, smarter, interesting, and more desirable than others who profess to offer what you offer. Then you have to be visible and promote the best of what you do. The best way to do that is to offer something no one else is offering.

Exercise 2: Mobilizing Your "Fan Base"

Make a list of those people who have the power to:

- Impact your career because of their position and influence
- Provide you with opportunities to be involved in high-profile projects
- Serve as a coach, mentor, or sponsor

Now, identify two opportunities that would help you to showcase your value and bring you greater visibility in your company.

Opportunity No. 1: _____

Opportunity No. 2: _____

3. Be a Servant Leader

The modern servant leadership movement was launched by Robert K. Greenleaf in his 1970 essay, "The Servant as Leader," in which he coined the terms *servant-leader* and *servant leadership*:

The servant-leader is first a servant. The servant-leader *is* servant first....It begins with the natural feeling that one wants to serve, to serve *first*. Then conscious choice brings one to aspire to lead. That person is sharply different from one who is *leader* first, perhaps because of the need to assuage an unusual power drive or to acquire material possessions.

In order to be a servant leader, you need the following qualities: listening, empathy, healing, awareness, persuasion, conceptualization, foresight, stewardship, growth, and building community.

A Moment of Personal Reflection...

I recently wrote a post for my Remarkable Leader blog in which I made reference to a comment that Colin Powell made about leadership.

According to the former four-star general and the United States' 65th Secretary of State, Powell stressed that the "true definition of leadership" is based on trust. And that the only way to gain trust is through serving selflessly as opposed to being self-serving.

Upon further reflection of the difference between serving selflessly and being self-serving, the story of Randy, a rising executive with a promising future, came to mind.

In 2009, Randy was scheduled for a major promotion when he was asked to launch a new division for his company. This project, which had to be completed within twelve months, represented a critical opportunity for Randy on many levels. To start, he would be able to demonstrate why he had earned upper management's confidence. In addition, he would then be responsible for a huge number of diverse reports, opening the door for expanding both his creditability and respect with those who would ultimately report to him once he assumed his new position. It seemed like the ideal scenario.

However—and this is where he came to the fork in the road that differentiates a selfless leader from a self-serving leader—Randy forgot an essential leadership quality. Specifically, he needed to be inclusive and recognize the contributions of others as absolute "must haves" in order to rally the team and reinforce management's decision to promote him.

Even though the project was successfully completed in eight months as opposed to the estimated twelve months—with an overall savings of $350,000.00—Randy did not understand the realities.

Following a brief celebration of the launch, Randy was invited into the CEO's office, accompanied by his boss. Expecting to be promoted, Randy could feel the adrenaline rush for an exciting future. Shockingly, Randy was told by the CEO, in an apologetic tone, that a search company was being hired to find the right candidate to run this new business. When he asked why he was being passed over, Randy was told that, based on the overwhelmingly negative feedback from those under him, there was no way he could effectively lead the division. In other words, he lacked a following. To quote the CEO, "Randy, no one wants to work with you again!"

In his self-focused agenda to successfully complete the project, Randy forgot about those committed individuals who gave selflessly to achieve success.

The moral of the story here is pretty clear. Randy used his team as a means for him to accomplish HIS goals, instead of being sensitive to their needs. He neither found opportunities to publicly acknowledge their contributions nor demonstrate his appreciation for their efforts.

"No man is an island." We are all connected to each other. A prerequisite for success today, we must always remember to choose selfless leadership.

An example of servant leadership . . . a brand that is sustaining

In the story of Randy, the rising executive, this attitude of servitude was definitely absent as he equated being a successful leader with producing results at the expense of establishing and nurturing relationships.

Now some may at this time be inclined to point to the bottom-line mentality that is seemingly so pervasive in the corporate world. What was it that Hall of Fame football coach Vince Lombardi stressed, that "Winning isn't everything; it's the only thing"?

While Lombardi, victorious coach of the NFL's Green Bay Packers for the first two Super Bowls, did indeed place a great deal of emphasis on winning, it was more in the context of being "relentless in the pursuit of victory." More specifically, Lombardi had "no tolerance for the half-hearted" player, nor anyone with a "defeatist" attitude. In truth, and as referenced in an online article by Jake Emen entitled "Vince Lombardi: A Case Study in the Art of Leadership" (July 2, 2007), the coach's success-oriented mindset was an extension of his unique ability to create "a compelling vision, establish shared values and encourage the heart."

In the same article Lombardi was quoted as once saying that "no matter how smart a leader may be," without the foundation of these key tenets, "he would never be followed by others or believed in."

This is quite the opposite of what many have come to think. While winning was the clear goal for Lombardi—as it is for any professional sports team—this objective was achieved through principles that actually reflected a servant leadership mindset. Above all else it should be noted that Lombardi's was a mindset based on *teamwork*!

Once again, this latter point relating to teamwork was something that Randy forgot on his way to "winning," in terms of successfully completing the project ahead of schedule. In essence, Randy became a lone gun. If someone is a lone gun, it's all about the competition—and winning. Even though they may initially be seen as bringing energy into a group, if they lack a team-building perspective, they ultimately risk being seen as a bulldozer. A person who is willing to push everything and everybody else out of the way in the pursuit of their "personalized" agenda, as opposed to working toward a "collective" goal, creates mistrust and discourages followers.

As Randy soon discovered when he was passed over for an expected promotion, winning without the contributions of others is indeed a hollow victory.

So what should Randy, and anyone who is in a position of leadership, do to foster the all-important balance between the pursuit of victory and servant leadership values? How can a leader pursue worthy goals that include rather than exclude and therefore alienate those with whom they must work?

To start, and assuming that you share and believe in the leadership values we have already discussed, you have to **consciously brand yourself as a servant leader**.

What is most amazing is that being seen as a servant leader is not based upon grandiose accomplishments. In truth, the best way to become a servant leader is by fulfilling your everyday responsibilities.

It is your day-to-day efforts that actually reflect who you are and for what you stand. In essence, to be a servant leader, you have to live your values through the sometimes small and seemingly innocuous actions that support and inspire those around you.

A good example of this immutable truth can be found in Frank Capra's 1946 movie *It's a Wonderful Life*. We all remember this movie with great fondness. In fact, it has become a timeless classic that airs every Christmas season, and has become an enduring example of how little things can mean a great deal.

Take the film's protagonist, George Bailey. While he aspired to doing great things—from traveling the world to building big cities—it was his daily contributions that made a difference in the lives of those who lived with him in Bedford Falls. Contributions, I might add, that served the interests of others.

Sadly, and like the aforementioned executive, George equated being outstanding with living big and living grand, when in reality it is the things we do every day that really count. He didn't recognize that through serving others he could achieve a level of success that few do. Consequently he considered himself to be a failure—until those whose lives he touched came forward to help him in his time of need. George Bailey, as it turned out, was indeed a servant leader, whose contributions were measured by the sum of every experience others had had with him.

While we will be covering the importance of becoming your best PR (public relations) manager in the upcoming chapter, here are a number of important tips that you can use to help you build a servant leader brand. In essence, follow George Bailey's example, and:

- Get others to see that you are interested in their opinions
- Be curious to learn how others see the same situation;

there is always more than one way to resolve a problem or implement a strategy
- Be more inclusive in your leadership style and draw out the contributions of everyone
- Go out of your way to recognize your colleagues
- Realize that you are not on your career journey alone, and allow room for others to be in the spotlight

Exercise:

List two ways that you could effectively demonstrate servant leadership.

1. _____

   _____

2. _____

   _____

4. Create Trust

There are key "best practices" for instilling trust. In order to be seen as a trusted brand you must walk your talk and hold yourself accountable to whatever happens. You must be aware of the fact that people will follow someone unconditionally based on their likeability, consistency, and trustworthiness.

The above paragraph succinctly and effectively highlights the core principles associated with being seen as trustworthy. The story in my following Personal Reflection demonstrates how these principles apply in the real world.

A Moment of Personal Reflection...

It is amazing how we all have a memory of something we did in which at least to a certain extent we continue to feel if not regret, then at least a disquieting sense that we could have done better.

From a personal standpoint, my moment of ruffled ease centers around a promise made but not kept.

The scheduling of a two-day seminar gave me a couple of extra hours to spare before having to leave for the airport. It was the Friday of a very busy week and of course I was eager to get home and relax over the weekend.

As I was packing up at the conclusion of my seminar, I was approached by a number of people who, while not included in the original session, asked if I might be willing to stay a little longer at the end of the day and provide them with advice on how they could better brand themselves.

Having a couple of hours, and always happy to help individuals who take the initiative to want to learn, I agreed to give them an impromptu mini-seminar before leaving for the airport.

Unfortunately, and in the intervening minutes between their request and assembling everyone, the HR person through whom the main seminar had been arranged indicated that she was ready to drive me to the airport.

When I had informed her of the employees who had approached me to spend time with them, and that I had agreed to stay longer, she said that I should not worry about it because they were not high enough in the organization to benefit from my expertise. She then insisted, despite my assertions that I had agreed to stay, that we leave for the airport right then. In addition, she expressed the need to get some personal coaching due to a challenging situation.

Against my better judgment I relented, and after letting the employees know that I would now not be staying, I left with the HR person.

A few weeks later, when I reviewed the attendee comments for the session with the same individual from HR, she also informed me that some employees had publicly expressed disappointment that I had left for the airport rather than honor my promise to stay and talk with them.

I was—and to this day, still am—disappointed in myself for not staying with the employees as I had promised. I had in essence gone back on my word and in the process damaged my trust relationship with them.

I, of course, agreed to visit the company again and a few weeks later delivered a free seminar to the disappointed employees.

But here is the point of this story . . .

Often we will encounter a situation in which for whatever reason we will feel pressure to go against our instincts and even our word as a means of diffusing conflict. It is at crossroads such as these that we must step up to the plate and remain true to ourselves and the words or promises that both build and maintain the trust relationship we have with others.

While it would have been easy for me to deflect by saying that the only reason I left was because of the pressure placed on me by the HR person, the fact is that when everything was said and done, I and I alone am responsible for my own actions.

In this context it is important to always remember . . . say what you mean, and mean what you say!

Colin Powell spoke of trust and how critical it is to leadership. He emphasized the fact that trust is perhaps the most important element in highly effective work teams, and that trust cannot be developed by any single behavior. According to Powell, trust, in its truest form, is a composition of many behaviors and their results that either increases or destroys a team's morale and therefore effectiveness. Ironically, **although a single action cannot build complete trust, one single action can destroy it**.

This is not to suggest that you always have to be right or have all of the answers. However, what it does mean is that even when you inevitably miss the mark (as we all do), it is how you handle the setbacks as well as the successes that solidifies people's confidence in you. The manner in which Johnson & Johnson handled the Tylenol crisis speaks directly to this point.

In the example I had presented based on my personal experience, no matter how much I would have preferred to go back and do it all over again, I could not "un-ring the bell." Rather than look for excuses as to why I did what I did or deflect responsibility by indicating that I had been pressured to go back on my word, I took full ownership for my actions. By doing so I was able to move beyond the original error in judgment and reestablish a solid rapport with an organization that is to this day a good client. Or to put it another way, while I cannot be expected to always be perfect—because no one can—I do however want people to know that I can be counted on or trusted to ultimately do what's right.

When it comes to assessing your trustworthiness, a careful self-examination does require a tremendous amount of personal courage. Being honest with yourself is the first step in deciding whether you need to change, and if so, what changes you need to make. After all, if we are not first honest with ourselves, then how can we be counted on to be honest with others?

Within this self-evaluative context, take a few minutes and complete the following quiz that explores trust and trustworthiness.

The Trust Quiz (A Question of Scruples)

Answer my "Trust Quiz" as openly and honestly as you can. You will find the results very revealing!

(Circle the number that corresponds: 0 = Never to 4 = Often)

1. I honor my word and follow through on commitments.

Never	Sometimes			Often
0	1	2	3	4

2. I say what I believe, based on my values.

Never	Sometimes			Often
0	1	2	3	4

3. I pride myself on being reliable and keeping confidences.

Never		Sometimes		Often
0	1	2	3	4

4. I always listen with purpose to show I am 100% present.

Never		Sometimes		Often
0	1	2	3	4

5. I always give people credit for their contributions.

Never		Sometimes		Often
0	1	2	3	4

6. I give honest and constructive criticism rather than avoid the facts.

Never		Sometimes		Often
0	1	2	3	4

7. I show respect for others regardless of their position or what they can do for me.

Never		Sometimes		Often
0	1	2	3	4

8. I take self-responsibility for my decisions rather than blaming others when something doesn't go well.

Never		Sometimes		Often
0	1	2	3	4

9. I honor teamwork and align my personal goals with team objectives.

Never	Sometimes	Often
0	1 2 3	4

10. I behave consistently, regardless of the person, the situation, or my level of stress.

Never	Sometimes	Often
0	1 2 3	4

TOTAL

How did you score on the Trust Quiz?

- **If your score is 30 to 40**: You are trustworthy beyond the norm.
- **If your score is 20 to 29**: You are trying to do too much to please others.
- **If your score is 10 to 19**: You need to level with yourself and assess vulnerabilities.
- **If your score is below 10**: You need to seek assistance in determining why you are setting yourself up to not be your "authentic" self.

Exercise:

Describe actions/behaviors that would help you to create and reinforce trustworthiness.

1. _____

_____

2. _____

_____

3. _____

_____

5. How to Be Courageously Consistent

One of the most important ways to manage the perception of your brand is by being consistent.

I have seen firsthand managers who treat their colleagues one way, their direct reports another way, and their senior leadership differently yet again. Have you ever worked with someone like that? People who do this are sometimes described as being good at "managing up," but that is rarely a compliment. What they are really doing is damaging their brand.

When someone observes you treating people differently based on perceived status, the first seeds of mistrust are sewn. They immediately start to wonder which one is the real you. As a result, you quickly become a brand they cannot trust. And **you can't build loyalty or a good reputation without trust**. Or to put it another way, what you need to do is to adopt brand discipline, which simply means that everything you do or say must remain consistent.

Think of brand discipline as being a "what you see is what you get" authenticity that isn't situationally based, but is constantly representing your values to those with whom you interact. Projecting a consistent persona creates a high degree of certainty and confidence in both co-workers and management.

Of course inconsistent behavior is not the only way to damage your brand's image and perceived value. In a 2012 Corporate Executive Board study titled "Open-Door Policy, Closed-Lip Reality," it was discovered that "nearly half of executive teams lack information they need to manage effectively because employees withhold vital input out of fear the information will reflect poorly on them." In other words, when employees remain silent or fail to speak their minds, companies lose on several fronts. For example, shareholder returns are 5.8 percent lower with those organizations whose employees are afraid to speak up. We are talking about hard, bottom-line dollars here!

For this reason, operating from the passenger's seat where you don't take responsibility for the direction of your business—where you purposely blend in with your surroundings and fail to venture an honest opinion, choosing instead to be "agreeable"—mutes your brand to the point of being nonexistent. This is what I refer to as being *consistently inconsistent*, whereby your behavior changes with the wind of popular opinion. While it may—at least for a time—keep you safe from controversy and potential conflict (and remember not all conflict is bad), it makes management question the value you are bringing to the business.

In fact, being a "yes" man or woman is actually more damaging to your career than being openly inconsistent in your behavior. This is because your opinions are not based on what you truly think, but on what you think the other person wants to hear. This leaves you in a perpetual state of having to seek approval or collaborate for the wrong reasons, rather than taking the risk to share your opinion. Eventually you actually become paralyzed in your day-to-day duties for fear that stepping out may be met with criticism. One thing is certain, either you or your company will tire of this veiled dance and you may find yourself burnt out and out of work.

Obviously, and as demonstrated by the above extremes, being inconsistent in your behavior or consistently inconsistent in your lack of expressing an honest opinion are surefire ways to sabotage your creditability, dilute your brand, and disappoint your organization.

So what can you do to determine where you are relative to establishing a trusted brand? The answer is simple. . . . Seek meaningful feedback from colleagues or a branding exercise partner by asking them the following three questions:

- *What am I doing right?* Inquire about where you are successfully projecting a consistent image and ask what behaviors contribute to that persona.
- *What should I stop doing?* Specifically ask which behaviors stand in your way of others seeing you as consistent.
- *What should I start doing?* Once you've stopped unproductive behaviors or mixed messaging, you'll have more time and energy for new behaviors.

Via the above research, you will gain an accurate assessment of the differences, if any, between how others see you and how you see yourself. You might even be surprised by the results, as they will most likely be enlightening. At this point, you can then begin to reconcile what behaviors to eliminate and the behaviors you want to adopt on a regular basis.

(Note: The last few paragraphs may seem as though we are going over ground that was already covered in the first chapter. You would, of course, be right. However, it is important that you seek feedback of this nature on an ongoing basis as circumstances as well as the people with whom you interact will frequently change.)

The following exercise will help you to assess the consistency of your brand.

Exercise:

- In what situations are you now willing to take greater risk or to speak out?
- Where can you now take on greater responsibility for the direction of your business?
- What can you be saying "No" to?

6. Be Specialized

In their 2011 annual report, Brand Finance listed the top 20 brands in the world based on their assessed value or worth. According to the report, specific sectors have fared better than others. For example, while the banking industry is seeing the continuation of a gradual recovery, consumer product companies such as Coca-Cola have seen the value of their brand fall by 9 billion dollars.

So why am I telling you this?

To start, the perceived value of a brand can and does change in accordance with how their products and services (areas of specialty) are perceived by the markets they serve. For example, in the 1960s through to the 1980s, Colonel Sander's Kentucky Fried Chicken was a highly successful brand that proudly promoted the eleven "secret" herbs and spices that went into its fried chicken. Beginning in the 1990s, as consumers became more health conscious, the brand's original strength began to lose its luster. In response to these external changes in consumer tastes, the company changed its name from the venerable Kentucky Fried Chicken moniker to KFC. As part of this major shift, KFC introduced healthier menu choices.

Then, based on yet another change in consumer tastes, KFC returned to promoting its fried chicken menu items. As a result, the Kentucky Fried Chicken name and logo were reintroduced in the US in April 2007 as part of a major rebranding strategy.

The point with this Kentucky Fried Chicken reference is that even though its brand image experienced several transformations over the years, its core specialty is and continues to be chicken. Go ahead and ask someone what comes to mind when you say KFC. Almost instantly they will say chicken.

In Chapter 1 I had made reference to the importance of managing your career as if it "were a start-up business." Similar to KFC, your "business" also has to have a specialty that enables people to immediately recognize your brand's value proposition. Therefore the key is to **identify your specialty and then effectively market it in the context of what is currently deemed to be a desirable or needed ability**.

This latter point is important. Can you imagine if KFC was reluctant to think outside of their familiar box? What would have happened if KFC put all their energies into promoting fried chicken instead of responding to public demands based on health concerns?

Recall the quote about insanity, which is defined as doing the same thing over and over again but expecting different results. How many of us fall into the trap of staying within our comfort zone to the detriment of not only ourselves but to those we seek to serve?

We may work harder or longer in the hope that we will demonstrate our value and in the process secure our position. But if we fail to adapt to changes the way KFC did, and insist on selling the equivalent of fried chicken when our organizations are looking for grilled chicken, our days will be numbered.

Whether you are self-employed or an employee, adopting an entrepreneurial mindset in which you act like your "own CEO" will steer you toward making sound decisions. It means that you will listen to what your "customers" are saying, and then position your unique capabilities to meet their interests and needs, all the while being true to your personal mission statement.

What Is an Entrepreneurial Mindset?

When you accept the fact that the concept of "job security" or "cradle to grave" employment are quaint notions from the past, you will begin to see your work as a series of temporary assignments in which your customer is the company that pays your salary.

This new "transactional engagement" mindset means that you are no longer tied to one employer but instead to those requirements and opportunities that lend themselves to best showcasing and complimenting your talents.

Is this a hard pill to swallow? Well maybe, but it has been a long time coming.

Dan Sullivan, founder of The Strategic Coach, Inc., began his business in 1971 as a strategic and personal coach when the term *personal coach* wasn't as much a part of the business lexicon as it is today. He spoke to the importance of having an entrepreneurial mindset when he emphasized the need for employees to become specialized.

From the infancy of his company, Sullivan, in his visionary brilliance, recognized that the concept of long-term job security would eventually become archaic. As a result, he believed that the way of the future would lead people to become *entrepreneurs*. To achieve success and distinguish yourself from the competition, he believed that you must first identify your unique ability and be able to articulate your value in concise messaging (i.e., a personal mission statement).

(Note: It is important to differentiate between a unique ability and an excellent ability—the latter of which I will touch on later in this section. Simply put, a unique ability is a gift or talent with which you were born. An excellent ability is a skill set that you acquire through education and experience. In other words, it is learned as opposed to being inherent.)

Adopting Sullivan's wisdom, you now have an exciting opportunity to build your enduring brand in a way that energizes you and sets you apart. By identifying what makes you stand out and defining your value proposition to your employer and/or customers, you will secure your bigger future using your best talents. You can also think of it in terms of adopting an "intrapreneurial" mindset.

Even though you are still technically speaking an employee, when you see yourself as an intrapreneur you will begin to think differently. Rather than simply fulfilling the requirements of your position, you will instead begin to think outside of the box.

With an intrapreneur mindset you will:

- See opportunities where none previously existed.
- Potentially change your goals and objectives as you embrace a new personal independence that will better align you with your organization's goals.
- Embrace your true unique ability because, similar to entrepreneurs, you will now be pursuing results

from a position of passion rather than just duty or job description.

- See the significance of advertising your unique ability because you know that it will help you to receive the recognition you deserve.

By adopting the intrapreneur mindset, any concerns you might have in terms of being seen as political will be eliminated. This is because, like any good business person, you will become strategic and intentional in everything you say and do.

In this light, the first and most important step is to ask yourself these important questions:

- What is my unique ability?
- For what am I best known?
- Why do people seek out my advice?

In providing the concept for the book *Unique Ability: Creating the Life You Want* by Catherine Nomura and Julie Waller (2009), Dan Sullivan refers to your unique ability as "the true source of your personal power which stems from those abilities you have that are unique to you."

Discovering your unique ability also allows you to rely on your strengths. And once you identify what's at the core of what makes you successful, you will now have "market positioning" because, chances are, no one does it as well as you. Based on leveraging your unique ability, your marketing position is now your specialty!

A Moment of Personal Reflection...

Do you underplay or undervalue that which comes most naturally to you? *If you don't work hard for it then it must not be great. It must not be a specialty.*

Unfortunately, far too many people either ignore or dismiss their unique ability, limiting their career opportunities by focusing on weaker areas that are oftentimes best delegated to others. (NOTE: refer to the Promoting Your Genius diagram.)

When I began my career, I aspired to spend it in fashion retail management. I was accepted into one of the most intense and thorough retail management programs in the industry. The downside of such an honor is that it created the illusion that I was suited to manage people. As a result, and for several years, in addition to running the business side of retail I was also mandated to build a solid sales force. This included being responsible for hiring, firing, and motivating a sales team.

If the truth be known, I was just mediocre at managing staff. I certainly knew it and perhaps my team did as well, especially given the fact that my passion for the assigned task waned when I had to push them to exceed their sales goals.

In this regard, my experience with one

particular company stands out.

Due to construction, a parking lot that was adjacent to the store was closed for several months. Consequently, traffic was reduced by more than 60 percent. Despite the circumstances, leadership continued to set high sales targets. I vehemently disagreed with these "unrealistic" targets and commiserated with the sales team for being placed in a no-win situation. Despite my misgivings, I was nonetheless mandated to fire low producers and pressure top performers to move more merchandise with high-pressure selling. Perhaps if I were highly competitive, I would have risen to the occasion.

However, my personal focus was on building my own clientele based on establishing a strong rapport and trust, and ensuring that customers were purchasing styles that best complimented their body shape and lifestyle.

After some deep soul searching, I had to admit that the "disconnect" between leadership's objectives and my personal values and goals meant that I was a lousy manager, in that I didn't know how to motivate a frustrated sales force. It took a couple of years more to finally acknowledge that management was not my strength and that my discontentment was being transferred to my staff. My work was at best mediocre and the days felt like they were getting longer and longer. My passion no longer existed and my energy level hit rock bottom. I became a mechanical manager in an energy-robbing role.

In retrospect, that should have been a warning for me to leave. I was doing a job, not living my dream.

So How Do You Discover Your "Unique Ability"?

In the famous song "Sixteen Tons" that was a worldwide hit for Tennessee Ernie Ford, he lamented the fact that after doing backbreaking work he only got "another day older and deeper in debt."

How many of us share those same sentiments about our present employment situation?

The fact is, that rather than capitalizing on our greatest strengths, we often take positions or pursue careers that do not provide us with the opportunity to showcase our real abilities and values. It is as if we are pre-programming ourselves to be just ordinary instead of extraordinary. So what's the answer, you ask?

Again, Dan Sullivan explains "unique ability" as an innate ability you were born with that gives you energy and a strong sense of personal fulfillment. While we all have special talents, Dan believes that this one unique ability, when showcased, allows us to distinguish ourselves naturally. And when you can differentiate yourself by your special ability, you will no longer have to worry about competition. As long as people know you possess this gift, you will be readily noticed and be sought out for your expertise.

Unfortunately, and as recounted in my Personal Reflection on page 60, we usually underestimate our unique ability or specialty's value because it feels so natural and easy to achieve. In addition, we are often encouraged to work at competencies that are weak so we spend less time enhancing our best attributes. Consequently, taking the time to identify this ability is usually put on the back burner so that we can focus on our weaknesses as opposed to our true strength.

My weakness, for example, was managing salespeople. Instead of focusing on building my own clientele based on my ability to build a strong rapport, trust, and provide sound advice, I was being asked to demonstrate success by initiating a high-pressure selling program. I would have risen to the occasion, but that is not who I am!

Originating with my mother, who was a top makeup artist, my unique ability and therefore specialty was not centered on getting people to buy what I wanted to sell. Because of her gift in helping people to reflect their true inner beauty, I recognized at an early age that how people looked and ultimately acted had to reflect their authentic selves. Sadly this did not align with the objectives of my employer, and thus I became frustrated and a little disillusioned.

Ironically, the majority of corporations are unlikely to promote individuals who invest solely in improving their weaknesses, yet these areas of improvement are always emphasized in a performance review. We then mistakenly believe that raising the bar in terms of our weaknesses will help us to move up. This, as I personally discovered, is a futile endeavor—especially if you have bigger dreams than simply keeping your job! When we compromise in this important area, we have in essence turned our "Genius Hierarchy" upside down!

How Are You Building Your "Genius Hierarchy"?

Of course your obvious question right now is, **What is a Genius Hierarchy?**

Divided into four distinct classifications or levels, your Genius Hierarchy is your personal competency scale through which you can identify and prioritize those attributes that lend themselves to best showcasing your personal brand's value. The first, about which we have already discussed at length, focuses on your *unique ability*. The second element is your *excellent abilities*, which you have perfected over the years due to experience, education, training, and repetition. The third consists of your *competent abilities*, with which you can get by but without distinction. The fourth component is referred to as energy wasters, which simply translates into your *incompetent abilities,* as they are a source of frustration and distraction and should be delegated.

Let's refer to the graphic below to illustrate my points and to help you to identify your greatest value and opportunity to differentiate yourself.

Unique Ability:

- Energizes
- Provides the highest level of self-satisfaction
- Such a natural talent that it seems to come easily to you
- Easy to negate because it feels like everyone would naturally have this talent
- Friends seek your advice because of this ability
- Success has come your way in life whenever you have used this ability
- You can use this ability all day long without getting bored or tired

Excellent Abilities:

- Provide you with satisfaction
- There are many rather than one or two
- These were developed due to experience and training
- Would not want to use these day-in and day-out because the degree of satisfaction would not be sustaining
- Reluctant to delegate them because you truly have excellence in these areas

Competent Abilities:

- You're good at doing these tasks but there is minimal satisfaction
- Tend to procrastinate
- No pleasure in using these abilities
- Most apt to put you in an unpleasant mood

Incompetent Abilities (Energy Wasters):

- You experience stress and frustration when using these abilities
- Not natural for you
- Take prolonged time to complete
- Put you in a foul mood—dissatisfaction with job
- Delegation is the only answer

Obviously, when you consider the above descriptors, it would be natural to gravitate toward those abilities that are unique and from which you derive the greatest satisfaction. This is, of course, a sound approach to promoting your specialty. However, you must learn to manage all descriptors or levels of your Genius Hierarchy. This includes maintaining your mediocrity at acceptable levels.

With regard to this last point, I have sometimes been asked if by placing the greater emphasis on doing those things that you enjoy and at which you excel encourages people to overlook responsibilities that are boring or difficult to do. In other words, am I advocating an "If it feels good do it, otherwise forget it" mentality?

Nothing could be further from the truth. The fact is that in business and in life there are going to be things that we have to do that in and of themselves fall into the Competent Abilities and Energy Waster categories.

I believe, however, that it is the big picture attitude that enables you to perform the less desirable tasks. Specifically, I may not like putting together a financial business plan. In fact, for me, this falls between Competent and Energy Waster capabilities. As painful as this process is, however, I can appreciate the comfort of knowing I have the ability to pay my bills, manage my time, and plan my income based on projections. I like the confidence

I derive from being proactive and benefit from the security that I have checks and balances in place, reassured that I am focusing on the bigger picture perspective, which ultimately enables me to function at the highest level of productivity.

However, I am very clear to delegate the implementation of my vision to those who possess either Unique Ability or Excellent Abilities in finance. For example, I have a full-time accounting firm managing my finances, an appointed bookkeeper for daily financial activities, in addition to a designated personal financial advisor.

Once again, I want to remind you that even if you are living your dream job, there will be times when you will have no choice but to participate in menial tasks. However, if you have been effective in delegating those tasks that you would classify as being Energy Wasters, you will at least be dealing with responsibilities for which you have some degree of competence.

> When you move away from the core of your intellectual property, you set yourself up for failure!

A Word Regarding Adaptability . . .

Similar to KFC, in which they responded to changing consumer needs by altering their name and introducing healthier menu items, your specialty must also have a certain elasticity. While you must remain true to the core principles of your mission statement, you must also be able to adapt your value proposition to meet the changing needs of your employer and customers.

I can remember how this point was driven home for me in a presentation on leadership by Colin Powell.

Powell, who is an American statesman and a retired four-star general in the United States Army, stressed that it is important to seek the advice of known experts. However he did so with the caveat that you should recognize the fact that some of these experts may have reached their peak in terms of their ongoing relevance. In short, being recognized as a thought leader will only matter if you can clearly demonstrate that your specialty delivers results for your organization in the here and now. This is an important point to remember.

Your past accomplishments don't speak for themselves! Longevity with your employer doesn't translate to the strength or value of your specialty. Remember the old adage "You're only as good as your last sale"? Your past work history is just that, and today's corporate mind has a very short memory. **To thrive, you have to keep moving forward and reinventing yourself as an indispensable player.**

As mentioned earlier, once you build a special reputation around your Unique Ability, you will be able to engage in activities that capitalize on your specialty, providing you with the greatest level of motivation and satisfaction. This is the true definition of an entrepreneur, and it is the practical demonstration of what you as an intrapreneur can bring to your organization.

Of course making the transition from employee to intrapreneur may also mean that you have to make potentially difficult changes. For example, what happens if your specialty, as defined by your Unique Ability, does not align with the goals of your employer?

While I am not suggesting that you give your notice at 9:00 AM tomorrow morning, it is a question that is worth serious consideration, especially since your level of motivation and satisfaction with what you do is directly linked to making a positive and meaningful contribution to your employer's success. This also goes for your customers as well.

If you hope to realize your greatest potential, you must take responsibility for seeking out positions in which you can use your Unique Ability. It's up to you to first showcase it. This will help you to become a valued resource and bypass those who are just doing average work.

Deciding on whether to stay with your present employer or seek out a new position with another employer will be a tough call. But unlike that rudderless ship I referred to at the beginning of this book, using your greatest talent will successfully navigate even the most treacherous of waters. This is all about committing yourself to a bigger personal future where you'll be operating from your best. You'll then be able to contribute at the highest level of productivity and contribute to overall progress for everyone with whom you work.

The following exercise will help you to determine where you should be investing your time and energies. Exploring your best capabilities will lead you to find your true calling. Once you can articulate your unique ability, you will then be able to promote your true value and build an unparalleled reputation.

To identify your Unique Ability:

- Recognize which areas and/or tasks provide you with a deep sense of self-satisfaction.
- Look for moments of excellence.
- Watch for behavior "flows" when performance is natural.
- Recall times when you felt energized while engaged in an activity or project.
- Consider the skills that sharpen the more you use them.

- Consider the skills that you have found effortless to attain.

Exercise:

Describe your Unique Ability using any of these openings:

- My unique ability shows up when I am . . .
- People seek me out when they need to know . . .
- I am most satisfied when I have the opportunity to . . .

If you are still unsure as to what your one special ability is, conduct market research. Ask the following question to approximately 15 individuals (selected from colleagues, direct reports, bosses, management, and customers):

"If you were going to open up your own company, what position would you offer me and why?"

This question is absolutely eye-opening. First it will allow you to see where they think you'll make the biggest difference and contribution to their company.

Second, you'll know if they see the best of what you have to offer. If they describe a role that you believe would minimize your value, they may be pigeonholing you or you may not be showcasing your best attributes. If you believe you have more to offer and they only see you from one perspective you will have to take stronger measures to market your Unique Ability.

If you want to further enrich this research, peel the onion deeper. When the individual shares the position they would offer you, ask them,

What qualities do I possess that make you see me in that position?

The key point to remember is that the time you invest will provide you with valid research and needed insight as to why your career or business may not be moving ahead at the pace you had hoped and expected.

7. Be *Courageous*

"Courage is not the absence of fear; it is acting in spite of it!"

While there are many versions of the above quote that express the same sentiment, it is the succinctness of Mark Twain's simple prose that has always provided me with an important touchstone whenever I have been confronted with a particularly challenging situation.

How do *you* deal with tough or uncertain situations? Do you procrastinate or pass the buck? Interestingly enough, when you do nothing you are actually making a negative decision. In essence, you are letting the situation determine the outcome rather than taking charge of your own destiny.

For example, what do you do if you hear that there is going to be a major layoff at your company? Do you hide and hope that you are not one of the people who will be sent packing? Or do you walk into the boss's office and let him/her know that you are interested in having a clearer understanding of the situation and what, if anything, can you do to solidify your position with the company?

Certainly, as demonstrated by the following story of Sheila, the latter not only takes courage in terms of speaking out, but also takes the courage to deal with the consequences of laying one's cards on the table.

"Act on clarity, not certainty." —Patrick Lencioni

Sheila was a top-flight executive who was being groomed for the chief position in her company when she was given the task of turning around the organization's failing European operation. Never one to shy away from a challenge, she accepted the difficult assignment. Within a relatively short period of time Sheila turned the company's lack of success overseas around, increasing revenues by 100 percent.

Based on her performance, one would assume that job security would not be an issue. After all, hadn't she dutifully, at the request of the American operation's senior management, moved her family from North America to Europe? Didn't she undertake an assignment that to most would have presented a daunting, high-risk endeavor that might have caused them to shy away? And didn't she deliver results beyond anyone's expectations?

Despite this glowing track record and the favor of her American bosses, when a new executive to whom she was to report in Europe was appointed, the unexpected happened. Within 30 seconds of their second meeting, Sheila was terminated.

How could this have happened? How could a smart, savvy executive who delivered extraordinary results suddenly be fired?

In her initial assessment of the situation, Sheila believed that the first meeting with her new boss was, in her words, "one of the worst first meetings" that one could imagine. In a follow-up call, and just prior to their second meeting, Sheila shared these feelings with this individual. Could Sheila's straight-forward dialogue have been at the root of her termination? After all, didn't he ask for her opinion? Apparently, at least with this new boss, such frankness was not only viewed in a negative light, it formed the basis for the dismissal of a top-notch executive.

At this point, you might begin to question the merits of stepping up and being heard. However, the fact that Sheila spoke up was probably the best thing that could have happened. As it turns out, her days were likely numbered prior to her first meeting with the boss.

Why, you might ask?

Sheila discovered that her new boss felt no loyalty toward her, as he had not initiated her transfer to Europe. Nor did he endorse her anticipated promotion. Thus he did not feel any obligation to keep her employed.

After the proverbial dust surrounding her firing began to settle, Sheila then discovered that her new boss had a friendship with another member of the management team who was about to be fired. Apparently, and after her success at turning things around, Sheila's expected promotion would have made this individual's job redundant. (Remember, prior to accepting the European position Sheila was being groomed for the top job.) Rather than seeing his friend outplaced, the new boss made the decision to fire Sheila instead.

So how is this better?

If Sheila had been less open and honest in her dealings with the new boss in terms of expressing her dissatisfaction with their first meeting, she might very well have held on to her position . . . for a time. However her boss, whose plans obviously did not include her, would likely have done everything he could to undermine her authority and ultimately her effectiveness and credibility. This would have ultimately been a far more destructive path. (See the series of articles I wrote on dealing with a "toxic boss" at http://remarkableleader.wordpress.com/?s=toxic+boss.)

Specifically, the key point to remember is not to wait until your reputation is destroyed and you have no choice but to leave. Instead, as was the case with Sheila, by speaking up in the manner that she did, she took control of the situation and was able to leave with her dignity and professional image intact.

As an epilogue, Sheila took control of the situation and not only received a fair financial settlement, her American bosses expressed their sadness at her unexpected departure. Sheila also landed on her feet from a career standpoint, being hired by a competitor of her former company whose innovative product line promises an even brighter future.

So what is the moral of Sheila's story?

Whether good or bad, events beyond your control will sometimes impact your career. Hiding in the shadows of obscurity only prolongs the inevitable, and in the process erodes both your reputation and motivation. As a result, it is better to **face challenges head on and let the chips fall where they may.** Certainly this will take courage, but the outcome will be in your hands rather than in someone else's. And isn't this the true definition of freedom and the ability to chart your own career course? Sheila knew this, and by living true to her values, she is now enjoying success in a new position with a new company.

A Final Word about Honoring Your Brand

In his book *Timeless Wisdom: A Treasury of Universal Truths*, Gary W. Fenchuk wrote, "According to the theory of aerodynamics, the bumble bee should not be able to fly. This is because the size, weight, and shape of its body in relation to the total wing spread make flying impossible. But the bumble bee, being ignorant of these profound scientific truths, goes ahead and flies anyway—and manages to make a little honey every day."

Like the bumble bee, it takes courage to go against the flow of popular opinion or difficult circumstances. However the reward for being true to yourself means that you (and your career) will take flight!

In those situations in which you will be required to speak up to ask for a promotion or present a new idea, the following formula will help you to speak with authority, inspiration, and courage.

The Influence Navigation Process

<u>Step One</u>: Be current in knowing what is happening in your department, company, and industry.

Identify what you are most concerned about if changes are not made. Be specific in identifying what the potential dangers are if no action is taken. Use logical arguments but also emotional arguments.

An example would be:

Logic: If the company does not take any strategic action, the competitors will have the edge. The value of our products will be overshadowed by the problems being experienced by our customers.

Emotional: This will instill mistrust by our customers, loss of revenue, and the possibility of having to downsize, putting all of us in a vulnerable situation.

<u>Step Two</u>: Identify opportunities you believe are feasible if the right action is taken.

Logic: We have the best talent. We have the best solutions. We have the best resources. We have the best demographics to tap into.

Emotional: If we capitalize on our personal strengths and take the risk to restructure our sales force, we can become inspirational leaders, and demonstrate our value to senior leadership.

<u>Step Three</u>: Give examples of the strategies you recommend with confidence and passion, and describe what will happen if action is taken.

Logic: I recommend that we set up three independent sales forces based on specialty, etc. In this way, our customers will have access to top experts in these areas of . . . We will then be able to not only recoup lost business, but expand into new and innovative initiatives that will exceed our target goals by . . .

Emotional: Everyone involved with this initiative will have a chance to feel refreshed, reinvigorated, and refocused on what will bring about significant success. As part of this winning initiative, you will be seen as essential to the business, making a difference while carving out your next promotion.

> "Courage is not the absence of fear, but rather the judgement that something else is more important than fear."—Ambrose Redmoon

Exercise:

1. What concerns you about how your business is presently being run?
2. What fears are holding you back from speaking up or from making key decisions to follow your intuition/ insights?
3. What needs to change in your organization and who can you reach out to who will not only listen but champion your vision?

So Tell Me, Are You Memorable?

Whether you are riding the crest of a recent success or toiling beneath the proverbial radar screen, one thing is certain . . . job security is an illusion. In this chapter I have tried to both dispel the myth of job security while providing you with a viable "take charge of your future" game plan.

Looking beyond Sheila's story and the fact that your past accomplishments don't speak for themselves, here are a few key highlights to remember from this chapter.

Align yourself with where your company is going. Just doing your job is not enough anymore. It's about creating a reputation for being the go-to person others seek out. Ask yourself: What are the major concerns for the future of your company? Where is your company going, and how can you align your value— your brand—to their bigger picture? How does the president of the company articulate his/her vision?

Be intentional by becoming skilled in those competencies that are seen as most valuable and necessary. By positioning your area of expertise as essential in building the business, you will be someone who people want to have onboard and follow. And by speaking the same language as your president, you will ensure that you are seen as a supporter.

Always be evolving. What gaps exist in your skill sets that you would need to fill to enhance your brand? Is it negotiation abilities? How about interpersonal skills or technical expertise? If you're the same as you were six months ago and you haven't learned anything new, haven't grown, haven't expanded your intellectual property, etc., you're going to quickly become outdated. There are too many smart people out there looking for jobs who do what you do. To avoid getting left behind, take courses or get a coach in areas where you have identified a skill gap. Be tuned in to business changes that may require shifts and offer fresh perspectives.

Networking matters. Never underestimate the value of building goodwill with your co-workers, even those you may not work with directly. Consider the case where you haven't built solid relationships with anyone other than your immediate boss. If he/she leaves, you're left with no one to champion you in your company.

You need to have an understanding of who the influencers are in your company, who is seen as having great value, and who has the ear of the president. Build relationships with these individuals in addition to those people to whom you are not presently reporting, as you never know who might be your next boss. The trick to being noticed and sought out for your expertise is to identify how you can bring value to everyone.

(Note: I will be discussing networking at length in the fifth chapter of this book.)

Key Tips from This Chapter:

1. Adopt brand discipline, which simply means that everything you do or say remains consistent.
2. You must be reinventing yourself when necessary, in addition to making yourself visible to key decision makers.
3. You must continuously be evolving and developing your skill sets for career opportunities.
4. Build your reputation by actively seeking activities that capitalize on your Unique Ability.
5. Relationships count and your ability to build them with key influencers will pay off.

Chapter 4—How to Be Your Best PR Person

"Many of us have been conditioned since childhood to think that self-promotion is bad and should be avoided at all costs. But tooting your own horn is no longer an option. Building a reputation for making things happen and being able to talk about it are critical to your personal brand."

When I had originally written the above for *The Leader's Edge* newsletter, it was a different time. We were in the earlier stages of the economic collapse. Everyone was, at the time, struggling to gain their footing in terms of assessing the impact that the declining fortunes of the markets had on their respective careers. Stepping up and standing out from the pack was not an option many wanted to consider, let alone pursue. After all, why draw unnecessary attention to yourself?

However, this is exactly what was called for as organizations looked for ways to cut costs while increasing individual productivity. Specifically, companies expected fewer people to take on increased responsibilities as workforces were pared down in an effort to save money. This meant that only those employees who could prove their worth in tangible ways were able to keep their jobs . . . at least for the time being. As covered in previous chapters, even those who had a track record of success fell to the "what have you done for me lately?" mindset. It became very apparent that rather than offering protection, remaining in the shadows meant that you were a much bigger target as marginal contributors were the first to be let go.

Today, companies take an even more strategically acute approach to business. This means that long-term projects have been replaced by task- or transaction-oriented assignments that have a definitive, near-future end date. Like firefighters moving from one blazing emergency to the next, personnel will, with increasing frequency, be changed as organizations seek out the best talent for the job at that specific point in time.

What does this mean to you, and in particular how you "sell yourself" as the individual most capable of helping your employer or customers achieve their project-driven goals? It means that employers no longer have the time to carefully sift through a resume or personnel file to try to extract your value proposition as it relates to their needs. In fact, and in the spirit of the Sun Tzu admonishment that most battles are won or lost before the fighting begins, if your organization's upper management doesn't know you or is not familiar with the value of your contributions, you are in BIG trouble!

This is why the first three chapters of this book are so important.

In the first two chapters you identified or perhaps clarified your beliefs and values. You then learned how to align how you see yourself with how others see you, including the value you bring to your relationships (and organization). Based on this process you were then able to create your personal mission statement.

Using your mission statement as your guide, Chapter 3 focused on creating a *memorable* presence or brand. Note my emphasis on the word "memorable."

You have to go through chapters one through three before you begin your PR activities.

Unfortunately, and as the following true story will demonstrate, going into "PR" mode when you have not built and promoted your brand effectively is almost always an exercise in futility.

A Moment of Personal Reflection...

Not that long ago, a company with whom I consult in the Far East underwent a major change at the top when their CEO suddenly left the organization. Shortly afterward a new Chief Executive was appointed and his first step was to determine who from his current executive team would continue with the company and who would be let go. To assist him in making this decision he scheduled a series of meetings with each executive, at which time they would present their vision as to where the company should go. The new CEO would then make his decision based on what he heard and how it aligned with his own visions.

Knowing that their jobs were on the line, each of these executives gave the best presentation of their life. They talked about their length of time with the company, what they had accomplished in the past, and where they saw the company's future.

However, despite giving it their all, the majority of the executives lost their jobs. The ones who kept their jobs had the benefit of knowing the lay of the land— or what the new boss wanted to see before they went into the meeting. They had this information because they had coaches who told them upon what areas they needed to focus, including how to align their vision with that of the new CEO.

Their PR efforts in the meetings were effective because they had recognized long before the change at the top occurred that to be successful in promoting their value (i.e., their brand), they had to have a solid understanding of their organization's inner workings. To get to this point, they networked with key people in their company, sought feedback as to their strengths and weaknesses, and were active participants in discussions. In other words, the platform upon which they would promote their brand was established and refined long before their meeting with the new CEO.

How prepared are you for the unexpected? Have you built a strong network of contacts within your organization, including individuals you would consider to be coaches and mentors? If you haven't, then there is no time like the present, because you just never know when you will be called into the meeting of your career.

Of course having reached this point in the book you have already read and incorporated steps one through four to Build Your Brand!

In this chapter, I will provide you with the tools to "get the word out" so that people will stand up and take notice. Or to put it another way, I am going to help you to become your best public relations or PR representative.

Isn't PR Fluff and Stuff?

Now I know that some of you reading this may be inclined to flinch backward with the question *Isn't it better to have someone other than me toot my own horn of accomplishment?* After all, no one likes a braggart.

You would be right in the context that nobody likes a braggart. But, being your own PR person has little to do with being a long-winded, get-up-on-a-soapbox-and-bore-everyone-to-sleep-with-your-conquests loudmouth. Unfortunately too many people for far too long have equated PR activity with a self-serving desire to hog the spotlight.

Although there are instances when a PR machine has elevated an unworthy product or person to the unwarranted heights of celebrity status, PR generally gets a bum rap. So let's start by redefining PR as **the means by which you can share how your Unique Ability can assist those you seek to serve in terms of getting them to where they want to go.**

The Starting Point . . .

In today's competitive and uncertain market, being your best PR person means that you have to continually look for ways to create career opportunities.

You may be wondering what I mean by "create" career opportunities. You may be asking how this is applicable to you given that you have been with your company for years! Why do you have to create a career opportunity? Haven't you already made an impression?

These are just some of the questions you may be asking yourself as you contemplate the need to do more than what you have already been doing. But (and isn't there always a *but*?), as we have already learned through the earlier chapters of this book, as well as perhaps even through your own experiences in seeing someone you know suddenly finding themselves out of work, no one is secure. And as pointed out in my story about Sheila in the section on courage in Chapter 3, true security is not based on tenure or expertise alone. Sheila landed on her feet with a new employer despite being wrongfully terminated because she understood her true value resided with her and not in having a position with a particular company. She also knew how to be a positive and therefore a powerful force for her company and those with whom she worked.

True job security means that you have to be proactive. It means that you have to seek out ways that your Unique Ability can contribute to a positive outcome for your organization, and if not with your present employer, then another. What it really means is that you have to adopt the intrapreneur mindset that I talked about in the previous chapter, as this is ultimately the starting point for your PR campaign.

So where do you start on this journey to create a career opportunity?

Your boss is usually the best person with whom to work in terms of identifying intrapreneurial opportunities within your present organization. In situations where your boss might not be accessible in this manner, you can also take the proverbial "bull by the horns" in terms of identifying opportunities to generate new avenues of revenue on your own.

I can recall the story about a personal computer manufacturer's sales representative who developed a very successful Employee Purchase Plan or "EPP" based on a simple yet innovative concept.

The representative saw that the majority of existing EPPs (for which the manufacturer's product was offered to client-company employees at a discount) rarely generated sales. While it seemed like an ideal venue, he wondered why so few employees took advantage of the program.

After extensive research, which was considered by many to be outside of his normal job description, the representative created an easy-to-order process that included guaranteed financing and convenient payroll deductions for employees. Within six weeks of the launch, the program generated more than a million dollars in high-margin sales. The program became so popular that it was introduced on a company-wide basis and ultimately grew to account for more than 25 percent of the manufacturer's revenue within an 18-month period.

Needless to say, the sales representative's ability to seek out and add a new revenue stream for his company provided him with rich rewards in terms of personal satisfaction, financial gain, and an opportunity for advancement. It also created a platform from which he could market his unique brand as an intrapreneur.

While you may not be in the same position as the sales representative in my example, there are still many opportunities to make tangible contributions within any given organization. Perhaps you may have an idea to streamline the manufacturing process. Maybe you can help to improve customer service or develop a new product. The point is that you have to look beyond your job description to see where your organization is in relation to where it wants to go.

This concept isn't limited to middle managers or the general workforce. This is also an encouragement to those who occupy the executive suite.

Be an Undercover Boss

In January 2010 the hit show *Undercover Boss* aired its first episode on CBS. The show featured then-President and Chief Operating Officer of Waste Management Lawrence O'Donnell III. O'Donnell went undercover within his own company to gain a better understanding of how upper management decisions had an impact on frontline workers.

The show became an immediate hit as O'Donnell, donning

overalls and hard hat, went from separating recyclables at a major plant to being fired from a position in which he was required to sift and pick garbage, to riding the back of a disposal truck. Since that first show, I have watched as senior executives from notable companies spanning all industries have themselves gone undercover in the quest to gain a better understanding of the companies they lead.

Besides being entertaining, I believe that *Undercover Boss* is a big hit because it shows that even those in the executive suite never stop learning and looking for ways to improve their companies. These CEOs who are lining up to be on the show never rest on their past accomplishments. They are always seeking out new and meaningful ways to make a difference. They are always networking and building new relationships.

For you, this last point in particular is important in that you never know who may become your next coach or mentor. As we discovered with my Personal Reflection earlier in this chapter, a coach or mentor will likely play a key role in how you position yourself in terms of demonstrating your value. And positioning is a big part of creating an effective PR strategy. (Note: In the upcoming chapter I will be talking at length about the importance of networking.)

As the CEO of your own company or brand, you are the manager and owner of your PR strategy. When you deliver tangible value and outcomes for others, you have to be able to talk about what you have accomplished in a manner that promotes your personal brand.

So within the context of the above, how do you toot your own horn without looking like a braggart?

> When you think about talking about your successes, begin to think about it in terms of sharing your success in order to make others successful.

Results Speak!

Like deeds, results speak, and they speak volumes about you. What have you done in the past few years that have caused others to shine? Have you come up with an idea or a vision that you took from concept to positive outcome? How have you motivated those with whom you work to achieve success in terms of their own unique abilities? These are the real credentials upon which you need to focus. This is also why the *Undercover Boss* shows are so interesting.

One truth that seems to emerge at the end of every episode is the gratitude of those employees with whom the boss has come in contact. They openly appreciate the fact that the person in charge has taken an interest in what they do, and has concern for their well-being. Besides having more motivation for their jobs, these employees invariably talk about the day their boss got in the trenches with them, and walked a mile in their shoes.

This mindset should be at the heart of your PR efforts. Specifically, you should be focusing on the impact your Unique and Excellent Abilities have had on others both within and outside of your organization. This is the best way to get people talking about you.

However, when you look at your accomplishments within

the context of how you have served the interest of others or contributed to their success, just relying on others to get the word out about you is not enough. You have to proactively look for opportunities to make a positive impact on those with whom you work and come in contact on a day-to-day basis. **Think of PR and personal branding as being a work that is perpetually in progress.**

Adaptable Brilliance . . . The Denise Foley Story

Denise is the Chief Procurement Officer and Vice President Purchasing and Payroll with AutoNation. Founded in 1996 by entrepreneur H. Wayne Huizenga, who is also the founder of Blockbuster Video and Waste Management, AutoNation is the largest auto retail company in the United States.

Over the past 16 years Denise has had 13 different bosses. Despite these changes at the top, Denise has been successful because she has been open to leveraging her Unique Ability to assume the leadership role within different areas of her company including finance, HR, and now purchasing.

To me she exemplifies the importance of volunteering for important projects, building an effective rapport with her bosses, and being willing to mentor and coach those with whom she works.

Having had the opportunity to share a cab with her to the airport from a speaking engagement in which she was in attendance, I was moved by her calm and certain demeanor that seemed to accentuate the very adaptability that has led to her enduring success.

Now you might ask yourself what Denise's story has to do with how you can become your own best PR person. Similar to those executives about whom I talked in my Personal Reflection earlier in this chapter, Denise recognized that while changes at the top can and obviously do happen, her success in promoting her brand value was based on a solid understanding of the organization's inner workings. When confronted with a change in management and company goals, Denise looked for ways in which she could become a champion of that change, even if doing so meant that she had to move outside of her apparent comfort zone.

In short, Denise realized that the new skills that were needed to play a different role in her company's success could be acquired through listening and building rapport with both existing as well as new team members. It is through this rapport and relationship-building process that Denise did her best PR work. And by adopting this attitude of service as opposed to being defined by a particular position, Denise established her reputation as a go-to person who could be counted on to take on the tough jobs and deliver the results.

> Effective PR is continually finding the spotlight... then shining it on others.

Helping Others

"Know where your market is headed and get there first—then write and speak about your successes indirectly by helping others." This key sentiment, which was expressed by one of my readers, is powerful in that it moves PR and personal branding from being perceived as an insincere, manipulative exercise to get ahead, to a servant mindset in which you have leveraged your Unique Ability to help others succeed.

Of course before you can help others succeed, you have to put yourself in the position to truly understand what it is that you can bring to the table. The only way to do this is to get involved.

For example, volunteer for high-profile positions or projects, or sit on important committees. You can offer to become a mentor or coach to a fellow employee, as well as schedule quarterly meetings with your boss to solicit feedback on what you can do to help him/her achieve their goals.

This last point about scheduling quarterly meetings with your boss is particularly important as it serves a dual purpose. Besides getting a better handle on what is important to your boss, it provides your boss with the opportunity to assess your value as a key member of his/her team. Many people get surprised at the end of the year when they receive a low performance rating. Being proactive means that your efforts are always aligned with your boss's objectives so that this doesn't happen. Once you have established a strong presence, you are able to focus or shine the spotlight on the needs and interests of others.

The PC sales representative with the EPP concept did not stand up on a pedestal and shout to the world, "Look what I did! I sold more than one million dollars of high-margin business in a matter of weeks!" He instead shared his success in the context of how it would help other sales representatives to succeed with their clients and prospects by following the same model that he developed. In this sense, **true PR and personal branding is one of drawing attention to what others can achieve with your help and expertise.**

You can now begin to "indirectly" write about and/or speak about your successes, leveraging what I call a Personal "Brag Bag."

So What Is a Personal Brag Bag?

A brag bag is quite simply your way of recording and sharing the "story of you," including your successes, in a manner that reflects your passion and ability to achieve results. It should include how you have helped others to succeed in the past, and how you are committed to helping them succeed in the future.

A brag bag can and should take many forms. For example, it can be the manner in which you answer the dreaded four-word invitation to "Tell me about you!" from someone you just met. It can be the way in which you describe yourself in a social network profile or write about specific subjects in a personal or company blog.

The essence of your brag bag can take the form of a personal bio that serves as an introduction to fellow members of a committee to which you belong, or to highlight your expertise as a speaker at a conference. Regardless of the venue, there is one thing that you must always remember . . . be consistent. When I say consistent, I mean that what you have in your brag bag must align with the experiences others have had with you. Or to put it another way, you have to walk your talk!

So . . . How Do You Brag?

From my own experience I know that there are times when it is essential for me to talk about my accomplishments in order to sell my services. Having walked the talk and delivered results for my clients I have reason to feel proud and to share my story. The key for me is to do so with both confidence and humility. This way I avoid coming across as being either self-centered or pompous. When you do this, you showcase yourself in the best possible light.

When I, for example, want to talk about my value to a prospect, I always say that I have the privilege to work with top talent internationally and feel a sense of pride when I see my clients rise to the top of their profession. Because my focus is always on what the client has accomplished through their association with me, I am getting my message out without sounding as though I am bigger than life.

> Even if you are at the top of your game, you have to self-promote.

Next to taking ourselves for granted and being convinced that we really haven't accomplished anything important, believing that others will naturally notice our hard work and reward us accordingly is a major misstep. Nothing could be further from the truth.

As mentioned earlier, you have to be proactive in terms of promoting your brand. In other words, do not get comfortable or overly confident with what you have done. Always look for new ways to excel and to leave your indelible mark. Then update your brag bag so that you can provide your present-day accomplishments in a credible and meaningful context.

The following ten questions will enable you to build your own Personal Brag Bag, which can then be adapted to any venue.

1. What should someone know about your history that would make you unique, interesting, and exciting to know?
2. Why do others attribute their success to you?
3. What would others say are five of your personality pluses?
4. What are the ten most interesting things you have done or that have happened to you?
5. What do you do professionally and why did you choose this type of work?
6. How does your job/career use your skills and talents?
7. What are you most excited about now in your profession and how does that best showcase your talents?
8. Of what career successes are you most proud (from current position and past jobs)?
9. What obstacles (professionally and personally) have you overcome to get where you are today, and what lessons have you learned from these experiences?
10. In what ways are you making a difference in people's lives?

Some Final Thoughts . . .

It is important to remember that a PR strategy or branding campaign is part of an overall package.

To me, branding is about creating a reputation based on who you are and what your value proposition is. A brand is based on how you showcase everything that defines you and will naturally differentiate you from others.

Above all, branding is about putting the interests of those you serve in the spotlight, so that when you help others to shine you will also bask in the reflection of their satisfaction with your contribution to their success.

Key Tips from This Chapter:

1. Establish an intrapreneur's mindset.
2. Seek out opportunities to create new avenues of success for both you and your company.
3. Create a Personal Brag Bag.

Brag Tips...

1. Document Accomplishments
2. Meet/Speak with Your Boss at Least Quarterly
3. Pick Important Committees to Join
4. Expand Your Resume
5. Teach, Mentor, Coach
6. Volunteer for High-Profile Positions
7. Become Indispensible

Section III—The Brand Building Strategy: Execution

We are now at the execution stage of our Build Your Brand Strategy. In this section I will focus on the practical application of everything we have discussed in the previous two sections, starting with networking.

I chose to start with networking for a number of reasons, including the important role it plays in laying the foundation for sustainable success. This includes establishing important links with both potential mentors as well as coaches. It also includes putting yourself in a position to get ahead of the curve in terms of new opportunities, whether within or outside of your present organization or industry.

Pay particularly close attention to Julie's story at the beginning of Chapter 5 to understand the importance of this last point.

Of course networking has taken on an added dimension with the advent of the Internet. However, I believe that networking in the face-to-face world has taken on even greater importance rather than being diminished by the convenience of the Internet. My reason is quite simple: Far too many people from the up-and-coming generational workforce have themselves been deprived of the opportunity to learn how to interact in person simply because they spend the majority of their time on the Internet. You must also consider the fact that, unlike any other time in history, businesses are likely to employ a workforce that is made up of up to four different generations at the same time.

Rather than creating an unbridgeable chasm in terms of communication, the next chapter will collectively demonstrate how networking in the physical realm actually complements networking in the virtual realm, and vice versa.

In Chapter 6 we will then review at length the concept of building your "find a need and fill it" legacy. More specifically, I will focus on how you can adopt a service mindset similar to that of AutoNation's Denise Foley (see Chapter 4) to ensure that you are always part of the changing business landscape of your company and industry.

With the title "Gratitude, Power, and the Meaning of Life," it would seem that the theme of Chapter 7 is somewhat self-explanatory. To a certain degree it is. However the unique insight you will gain from this part of the book will come from the real-life stories that provide living examples that are certain to resonate with you.

In the final two chapters of our shared journey together, you will hear from some of the business world's most notable experts and thought leaders regarding their experiences and views on how to build an enduring personal brand.

In conjunction with what we have already covered in Sections I and II, this third section will serve as your doorway to realizing your greater future . . . the future of you!

Chapter 5—The Importance of Networking

"Your network is your net worth."

Even before the emergence of social networks and social media, to many, the idea of networking was a necessary evil. Mistakenly viewed as a distasteful exercise in self-promotion involving feigned interest and superficial pleasantries, most either limited their interactions to a peripheral involvement or shied away from networking events completely.

While there are perhaps any number of reasons for the bad press associated with networking, two things are a certainty: expanding your network is not an option, and the ability to network effectively begins with a proper view of what it involves.

It is interesting that there are no shortages of books, audio books, and other reference material designed to help people become better at networking. The irony is that all the expert advice and insight means very little if you view the exercise in a negative light. For this reason I am, in the first part of this chapter, going to focus on helping you to see networking in its true light. I intend to remove the forest of misperception so that you can finally see the trees of opportunity.

Don't Wait for It to Rain . . .

I recently had a conversation with a longstanding client. Having just missed being one of the many who found themselves out of work when his Fortune 500 company downsized, he reminded me of a discussion we had not that long ago about the importance of networking. At the time I had cautioned him "to not wait until you need a network to start building one." My words returned to him time and again as he thought of who he might call to land another job if he were among those the company decided to let go. While he dodged the proverbial bullet this time, the fact that he had taken my advice and built a strong network of contacts meant that he had a number of options had the worst happened.

In this way, **think of your network as being your "in case of emergency" career contact list.**

I can think of no other example in which the emergency concept was more applicable than it was with Julie.

Career 9-1-1

For 15 years, Julie held a senior position within the healthcare industry as an event planner. Overseeing her company's venues in both the United States and Latin America, she had built a tremendous reputation for being an on-the-ground, front-line manager whose presence at exhibits and events exemplified the term "personal service."

In essence, she was the face of the company, welcoming guests and attendees, responding to staff needs, and overall doing what any exceptional event planning manager does . . . creating a positive and memorable experience for everyone involved. (This also included the members of her event team.)

Having come through unscathed in an acquisition and subsequent merger of two divisions into one, it is safe to say that what happened to Julie when her company was most recently acquired caught everyone by surprise. She was blindsided, as she found herself suddenly out of work.

It is hard to say why, in this particular instance, she became the odd person out, especially since she had made every effort to become part of the new event planning team. But like Sheila, whose story I shared with you in Chapter 3, there are oftentimes circumstances beyond our awareness and control that can conspire to undermine our position. Once again, this is why no one is truly safe in terms of job security.

Despite a glowing track record and having strong relationships with members of her original company's senior management, Julie still found herself unemployed.

When I spoke with Julie shortly after her dismissal, she reflected on the fact that the network she had built was for her a port in a storm. Besides receiving great emotional support from everyone with whom she had interacted and built rapport with over the years, Julie discovered firsthand how valuable her network was in terms of getting the word out that she was now available and looking for a new position.

Even though the disappointment and hurt at being cast aside after 15 years was still fresh, Julie did not use her network to vent or to point an accusatory finger at those she believed may have been responsible for her dismissal. Instead, she graciously thanked those who contacted her and asked them to keep her in mind should they hear of an opening at another company. Her network also became an important resource in terms of providing guidance and expertise on how to deal with the dismissal and how she might better her chances of finding the right position with a new organization.

Like the old axiom that people do business with someone they know, like, and trust, those who hire will be more inclined to give greater consideration to someone who they know or who comes to them by way of a referral from a trusted connection.

The fact that Julie had been building a strong network over the years meant that she was not starting from a position of being familiar to only a close or limited circle of contacts. This means that similar to Sheila—who herself landed a great position with another firm after she was suddenly dismissed from her job— Julie's prospects for landing on her feet were also promising.

A Happy Ending and New Beginning for Julie

Just a few short weeks being let go, I received a message from Julie indicating that she was going to be starting her new job the following week.

As the new Associate Director of Commercial Operations with a pharmaceutical company, Julie would be heading up a department that included a team of five planners responsible for managing the company's meetings and trade shows.

In fact, in highlighting the following chain of events that led to this new beginning, Julie's experience speaks to the interconnecting powers of one's personal network of contacts:

1. While still employed, Julie mentioned to a colleague that she was interested in a job she had seen posted at another pharmaceutical company.
2. This individual told her that a mutual colleague's wife was a Senior Director at that same company. The mutual colleague's name was Pat.

---

3. As Julie knew Pat well, she was able to talk with him honestly about her job search, and asked if he would mind passing along her resume to his wife, which he did.
4. Ironically, in the following weeks, Pat resigned and left their company.
5. Shortly thereafter Julie was laid off.
6. Julie e-mailed Pat to let him know that she was no longer with the company, and she followed up the e-mail with a phone call, during which time they had a chance to talk at length.
7. A few weeks later, Julie saw the posting for the Associate Director position at the company where Pat's wife worked.
8. She sent another message to Pat, and he suggested that Julie talk directly with his wife, Carolyn, who, as previously indicated, was the Senior Director.
9. She met Carolyn for coffee, at which time Julie provided Carolyn with her resume. In submitting Julie's resume to her company's HR Department, Carolyn spoke to Julie's strengths as a candidate for the position.
10. Shortly afterward Julie went through a series of interviews and... she got the job.

There is no doubt that Julie's qualifications, which were clearly demonstrated in the series of interviews with the company's HR Department, is the reason why she landed the job. However, without leveraging her network as effectively as she did, the door of opportunity to demonstrate her qualifications may never have opened.

This is the reason why your network is, in reality, reflective of your net worth!

So What Is the Real Problem with Networking?

Given Julie's story, as well as those of countless others whose networks are their ports during a career storm, the real question is, **Why don't people network?**

Similar to public speaking, the idea of networking often presents an ominous obstacle, as it usually requires you to do something that is outside of your comfort zone. Specifically, you have to initiate conversations with people you do not know or about whom you have only a passing knowledge. The difference from public speaking is that, instead of sometimes having to get up before a large audience of several hundred to establish rapport, you need approach only one individual or a small group of people.

As someone who has had the privilege of addressing audiences of all sizes the world over, it is natural to have what I call the "pre-podium butterflies." Rather than deny this natural fight-or-flight instinct in networking situations, the first step is to acknowledge your resistance and even embrace it. Only then will you be able to deal with it. Or to put it another way, you are not alone in how you feel. In fact, the person or persons with whom you are going to connect at the next networking event are probably experiencing those very same feelings as they see you approach them from across the room. This is why one of the golden rules of effective networking is to focus on the other person and their interests. When you ask people to talk about themselves and their interests and passions, they will almost always drop their guard and open up to you.

The key point here is that, by sincerely focusing on learning more about other people, you will make a positive impression in that you are making them the center of your attention. Once they have told you something about themselves, they will invariably ask you to share a little bit about yourself. Make sure that you have your own Personal Brag Bag ready. (See the previous chapter.)

Now you can start to see networking in a whole new light—or in the case of this chapter, the trees have been removed so that you can start to enjoy the entire forest!

Look at Networking as an Opportunity

Networking is all about creating and sharing opportunities. The more authentic you are, the more resilient and valuable your networks will become. Regardless of being introverted or extroverted, you can still maintain your authenticity and be true to yourself if your focus is on the shared value that you bring to your relationships. Perhaps the best question to ask yourself is, **Why would someone benefit from being connected or associated with me?**

Don't Be a Networking Snob

As alluded to earlier, the challenge for some people is that they confuse networking with being insincere or fluffy. Sometimes this perception is just a cover for social insecurity, or even laziness. To make any meaningful progress in terms of building your personal network, you have to have a heart-to-heart with yourself. Or to put it another way, the sincerity (or lack thereof) of the networking process resides completely with you! If you are sincere, then you will build a strong network based on solid networking values.

Once again—and it is worth repeating—**when you learn that networking is not about you but rather the value you create for others, you'll embrace the opportunity to meet and connect with people because you will be able to share resources, offer advice, and have fun.**

No Beginning and No End

If you think your network is a one-way street to benefit only you, then you are mistaken. Call it your "professional" network and look at it as a circle—with no beginning and no end. The help that you give to someone today will come back to you when you need assistance or support. It is truly a case of "what goes around comes around." This is not to suggest that you give only to get. Rather, your network is, in reality, one of reciprocal arrangement whereby everyone benefits.

Information and Connection

"Knowledge is power!" How many of us have heard this saying over the years without really appreciating its full meaning and impact? Yet today, being an information broker is a hot career path for a growing number of people—with big financial rewards.

I am not suggesting that you leave your present job and hang out the information broker shingle. What I am saying is that you can still stand out as a master networker by offering your contacts the same value. To start, share information with a generosity of spirit. If you have details that you know will be helpful to others, let them know about them. By doing this, you will naturally enhance your value.

Do you know people who would benefit from your network? Become the ultimate matchmaker by facilitating introductions between your connections. Matching people who can derive value from a relationship you brokered demonstrates your thoughtfulness and desire to help. Simply put, combining information with connection sets you apart. Who do you know right now who wouldn't want to be privy to your help?

Adopt Host Behavior

For years, I have been preaching the importance of creating a stronger presence in the business arena. One of the most effective and easiest ways to do this is to adopt a host attitude or behavior.

A host is an empowered person who makes others feel welcome, comfortable, and important. A host can anticipate how others expect to be treated—the old golden rule of treating others the way you would like to be treated immediately comes to mind. You can enhance the experience by taking this a step further. Adopt the platinum rule and treat people *better* than they expected. You are guaranteed to stand out from others!

Hosts know that no one wants to feel embarrassed or uncomfortable, or to be made to feel wrong. As a host, you create a nonthreatening environment that encourages others to respond to your ideas by making them feel that you are truly listening to what they have to say.

Like any great host, making small talk and putting others at ease sets the tone for any meeting. Regardless of your position, acting like a host will serve you in that it will allow you to showcase the best of who you are at all times.

Build an Internal Network

Do not limit your rapport to only a select group of people. If you develop a connection with colleagues but do not have rapport outside your department, you may shortchange your career. If you connect only with the customers you serve and not with your colleagues, you may find there is no goodwill at "home," where you may need it the most.

Having access to a bigger network gives you greater opportunities to seek out sponsors for your ideas and projects, in addition to gaining different perspectives. In turn, you can reciprocate by offering to showcase their projects to your direct network. Think about this alliance as making a withdrawal from your bank without ever needing to make a deposit. Increasing your visibility strategically will earn you a higher profile within your company. It also will help to prevent you from getting pigeonholed in a job.

Expand Your Network

Aside from seeking to network with people you already know, how are you expanding your network to include those with whom you are unfamiliar? For example, seeking opportunities to volunteer for projects where you may not know the individuals involved will serve you well by expanding your sphere of contacts and influence.

Of course, the majority of "networking resisters" seek the comfort of familiar contacts as opposed to building rapport with new people. Unfortunately, your influence and brand are only as wide and as strong as the circle of people within your network. Limit your network to just a few and you will be limiting your opportunities. My best networking has been when I have volunteered to speak at an event where I did not know anyone! This forced me to meet others which, over the years, has led to lasting relationships.

Extend Your External Network

A great way for getting more involved in your industry and expanding your circle is to research professional organizations in your field. Consider local clubs, college alumni associations, conferences, and charities. While offering great programs and educational opportunities, associations such as these also provide the perfect venues through which to meet others.

Start by making a list of everyone you know, need to know, or want to know better within your industry. Then trace old colleagues who could help facilitate introductions. The key is to get out there!

Getting Ready for a Business Networking Event

Prepare, prepare, prepare!

In advance, invest time in researching topics that are conversation openers. Doing the research will be a confidence builder. Anticipate with whom you will be meeting, or the type of people attending the event. Choose topics that will allow you to establish commonality. Usually human interest stories work if they do not involve controversial subjects such as race, religion, abortion, and politics.

For those you know you will meet, research something about the person's recent achievements, such as a promotion or an important new client. If you can't speak specifically about the person, know something positive about the company he/she works for. A trick that I use prior to meeting someone is to see if we are connected on LinkedIn. If so, I note the associations or groups with whom they are affiliated. This provides me with additional information as to their interests. I also make it a point to read the testimonials others have written about them, which provide me with even greater insight into how they have impacted the lives of those with whom they have come in contact.

Above all, treat the person as your guest. As I said above, when you assume a host behavior, you will naturally project greater confidence and warmth.

Perfect Your "30-Second Elevator Pitch"

When you meet someone for the first time, and after hearing a bit about them, it is now your turn to tell them the story of you. Your goal is to be able to build and hold rapport with them as you speak about yourself in a compelling way. To do this effectively, you need to have an amazing 30-second elevator pitch!

Elevator pitches are savvy marketing tools that tell your story in less than a minute. Here are just a few examples for you to consider:

Leadership, image and branding specialist: Hello, I'm Roz Usheroff, and I have the privilege to work with top talent globally to help executives expand their personal power and leadership.

Investment and insurance advisor: Hello, I'm Brian Ashe. I get to help families live out their dreams by advising them on sound financial investments. Not only do they get to see their portfolios grow to their expectations, they feel greater peace of mind about what their future will look like.

Marketing director: Hello, I'm Stu Cheung. I develop innovative/integrated marketing campaigns to support my organization's corporate brand. This helps improve patient care, which really motivates me to do what I do.

Notice how with each pitch there are no titles. Focus instead on your products or services and let the listener hear how your expertise benefits others. Specifically talk about the challenges and risks that you have enabled your client/company to avoid and turn into a positive. For example, you can see that Brian helps clients feel an increased level of comfort through proper financial planning. Stu, on the other hand, focuses his energies on improving the care that patients receive. It's as simple as that!

A compelling, attention-grabbing pitch tells who you are, the value of what you do, and sells that to anyone, internally and externally. If you capture their attention, you will have an opportunity to distinguish yourself from others. You will, in other words, become memorable for all of the right reasons!

So how do you craft your 30-second elevator pitch?

1. Highlight your value proposition . . . immediately.

Whenever we meet new people, there is a tendency to question whether this is someone I want to know better. Most are not as interested in you as in what you can do for them. Call it the classic law of "What's in it for me?" Focusing on the benefits that people will experience from either knowing you or working with you will inspire others to say, "Wow . . . tell me more!"

2. Keep it short and succinct.

I do not want to know your life story. Avoid a cluttered elevator pitch that sounds boring and painful to listen to. This is not meant to sound like your job description.

3. Don't mention your title or company name at the beginning.

Defer discussing your actual job or company until after your pitch. You're talking about you, so be careful to make the focus on you first, not the company. If the focus of attention is on your company, know that people will not listen to your intro without judging your company first. Refrain from using your title on your business card. It can be misleading, as it never describes all that you do.

4. One size does not fit all.

Remember, your 30-second elevator pitch is designed to stimulate further conversation. Do not get locked into what I call a "conversational script" in which you paint everyone with the same brush. Having listened to what the other person has said about himself, align your pitch with his interests.

Take my pitch, for example. Let's say that the woman with whom I am talking has indicated that she has just been asked to head an important project within her company. After delivering my pitch, I would follow up with a comment about how in my role as a leadership, image and branding specialist I have helped people in similar circumstances achieve greater results. I would then ask her what her goals are pertaining to the project, and what she sees as being the biggest challenges in terms of achieving her desired outcome.

5. Remember the mutual acquaintance factor.

If you follow the recommendations from the Getting Ready for a Business Networking Event section (see p. 113), you will undoubtedly discover the existence of mutual or shared connections with the person with whom you are talking. This is a powerful advantage in that moving in similar circles and knowing some of the same people establishes your credibility even further. This is especially true if someone they know is already working or doing business with you. Think of it as a seal of approval in which the other person is likely to think, *If you are good enough for Joe, then you must be good at what you do.*

6. Use family and friends to rehearse.

You want to sound natural, excited, and authentically you. You do not want to come across as an arrogant one-of-a-kind genius, nor do you want to look and sound submissive. Therefore the way you fine-tune your elevator pitch is to seek feedback from others who know you.

In the end, you've hit a home run with your 30-second elevator pitch when you are invited to provide more information, or when the other person replies, "I could really use someone like you in my job!"

So next time you find yourself at a business function where you want to begin a meaningful conversation, here are some easy tips to follow:

- *Relax.* Everyone else is as nervous as you are about meeting strangers.
- *Approach people* who are standing alone with a warm smile. They will be relieved that you reached out to them. Or, approach a group of at least three people. They will be less likely to be engaged in a personal conversation than just two people. To break into a conversation, simply say, "Excuse me for interrupting, but I wanted to say hello and introduce myself."
- *Be the first to initiate the handshake* that says "I am a confident person who is happy to meet you." Make it memorable by holding on until you register the color of their eyes, then let go.
- *Do your homework* if you know who you are meeting. The more you invest in research about an internal or external customer, the easier it becomes to establish commonality.
- *Keep yourself current.* Make it your business to know what is happening in the scientific and business communities, and on major news items, sports stories, and popular TV series.
- *Avoid looking like an interrogator* for the FBI/RCMP. You will close down most conversations if

you start punching out too many questions that begin with "Do you...?" or "Are you...?" or "Have you...?" The goal of initial questions is to start a dialogue. Be prepared to answer the same questions you ask.

- To feel comfortable, *always be prepared* with two questions or talking points beforehand. Genuine open-ended questions that allow the other person to provide information will help conversation flow. Ask about projects they are working on, trips they're planning in the future, or activities they enjoy.

- *Be genuine.* Allow yourself to be open and offer some personal information that would make the other person feel comfortable. I am not referring to details about your "intimate relationships," rather something about your kids, your passions, etc.

- Use this opportunity to *share what you do* and any recent accomplishments so you gain the appropriate credit. When delivered in a conversational style, you are ensuring others that you know what you are doing. When you provide explicit details, you are making sure that others won't be able to take credit for what you have done.

I encourage you to get out there, physically, into the world of opportunity. IPhones and iPads can never replace a handshake, a warm embrace, or an inviting smile. They are powerful tools, but they are not a substitute for human conversation over lunch or at a network event where you can share your results.

Networking is no longer optional for those individuals who want to control their destination. If you hide behind excuses like having "no time," you are not taking advantage of opportunities to naturally showcase your work. If you physically hide yourself, you make it easier for others to stand out and become associated with projects for which you deserve the credit.

Follow Up with a Personal Touch

What you do *after* meeting others is vital. Send the person a handwritten note—invest in a good fountain pen and some buff-colored stationery as a symbol of good taste. This is one time when an e-mail won't do.

If, in the course of your discussion, you learn something about the person—she is an avid golfer or he collects art—be on the lookout for interesting articles to forward to them occasionally. Or, if you read something related to their job or industry, send that along. Besides being an excellent way to refresh their memory about you, it also sends the message that you were listening to them. After all, and as my grandmother used to say, we were given two ears and one mouth for a reason. People like to be heard, and even more importantly . . . remembered.

Social Networks: Become Part of a Community of Shared Interest

Becoming part of a community of shared interests and mutual gain, whether in the real or virtual realms, is something toward which we all strive.

Do you recall the falling tree thought experiment that was originally presented in the 1910 book *Physics*, by Charles Riborg Mann and George Ransom Twiss? For those who may not know it, it poses the philosophical question, "When a tree falls in a lonely forest, and no animal is nearby to hear it, does it make a sound?" As is the case with the "tree falling in the forest" analogy, you may have a great deal of knowledge and practical expertise; however, what is the point if you fail to connect with those who can benefit from what you have to contribute?

In conjunction with your everyday networking activities in the physical world, social networks such as Facebook and LinkedIn provide you with an unprecedented ability to rapidly expand your reach in terms of sharing your brand value with a global audience. After all, potential employers and customers tend to check out people before agreeing to meet them in person.

Of course one of the great things about social networks is that they are easily accessible from your office at work or your den at home. Another advantage is that many find that meeting and talking with people on LinkedIn or Facebook is less daunting, as they are operating from a position of familiarity or comfort.

There are many books about how you can best leverage social networks to get your story out there. So while I will leave it to you to do your own research in this area, I will end this section with a cautionary note: Make certain that your subject matter and manner of interaction online is in line with your true values. Or to put it another way, make certain that all of your interaction on networks is in line with the image you want to project. This includes your profile picture as well as the posts you share with your connections.

I can recount many stories of when a person's Facebook profile or tweets on Twitter cost them their jobs. One example in particular stands out. This individual had just landed a new job and tweeted that while he was happy to have won the position, he considered it to be a temporary move until his dream job became available. Unfortunately, his new boss was also on Twitter, and after reading the post he immediately retracted his offer of employment.

Remember, in the virtual realms, once something about you is out there . . . it is out there *forever*!

Assess Your Networking Skills

So, what have you learned from this chapter? Are you a network master . . . the ultimate information broker?

Take a few minutes to complete the following quick quiz to find out.

Network Assessment Exercise:

Circle the number that represents your present achievement level.

1 = Never   2 = Rarely   3 = Sometimes
4 = Often   5 = Always

1. When I meet new people, I engage them right away.

Never	Sometimes		Always		
0	1	2	3	4	5

2. I'm comfortable joining a group of people who are already talking.

Never	Sometimes		Always		
0	1	2	3	4	5

3. I network at least two hours a week, both internally and externally.

Never	Sometimes		Always		
0	1	2	3	4	5

4. I am well connected to the most powerful people in my company.

Never	Sometimes		Always		
0	1	2	3	4	5

5. People call me to help them make a connection.

Never	Sometimes		Always		
0	1	2	3	4	5

6. People like me and seek out my friendship.

Never	Sometimes		Always		
0	1	2	3	4	5

7. I have a great 30-second elevator pitch to introduce myself.

Never	Sometimes		Always		
0	1	2	3	4	5

8. Before I go to an event, I prepare small talk on specific resources, tips, and trends.

Never	Sometimes		Always		
0	1	2	3	4	5

9. When networking, I am good at circulating within the room.

Never	Sometimes		Always		
0	1	2	3	4	5

10. Soon after a networking event, I reconnect with two or three people I talked with.

Never	Sometimes	Always
0 1	2 3	4 5

11. When I forget someone's name, I know how to deal with the situation comfortably.

Never	Sometimes	Always
0 1	2 3	4 5

12. I know how to end a conversation comfortably and professionally and move on to the next person.

Never	Sometimes	Always
0 1	2 3	4 5

13. I initiate at least one networking meeting (breakfast/ lunch) a week with a colleague.

Never	Sometimes	Always
0 1	2 3	4 5

14. I choose to eat in the cafeteria where I can circulate with a group of people.

Never	Sometimes	Always
0 1	2 3	4 5

15. I know how to increase my visibility within my organization.

Never	Sometimes	Always
0 1	2 3	4 5

16. I can say exactly how my internal/external networking activities have paid off for my career.

Never	Sometimes	Always
0 1	2 3	4 5

TOTAL

How did you score on the Network Assessment Exercise?

- **If your score is 70 to 80**: Continue your great work at networking.
- **If your score is 60 to 69**: You're doing well, but you can intensify your efforts.
- **If your score is 30 to 59**: You're missing out on opportunities. You need to meet more people—or hire a publicist!

If you are already well connected, then keep on doing what you are doing. After all, networking is an ongoing process in which the introduction of new people into your growing circle of contacts is a must. Conversely, if you are one of the many who need to get out in the networking world more, avoid making excuses for not engaging with others, as you just never know from where your next job or business opportunity will come!

Key Tips from This Chapter:

Remember, don't build a network that looks like you. Diversify! Step out of your comfort zone to connect with different types of people. Think about networking as booking time to make a difference to others.

When it comes to networking, the old adage of "what goes around comes around" has never been truer than it is in this challenging economy.

Here are a few more key tips for you to remember:

1. Networking is not (nor has it ever been) optional!
2. Whether in the physical or virtual world, the same rules apply.
3. Ask not what your contact can do for you . . . add value as a connection.
4. Like the famous advertisement . . . with networking JUST DO IT!

Chapter 6—The Find-a-Need-and-Fill-It Legacy

"Find a need and fill it!"

So states Ruth Stafford Peale, wife of *The Power of Positive Thinking* author Norman Vincent Peale.

Powerful and insightful in its very simplicity, it reminded me of an article by Jon Hansen titled "Rosslyn Analytics: Find a Need and Fill It!" In the article, Hansen lamented the fact that the true meaning of this axiom is surprisingly and consistently overlooked by the majority of organizations.

Referencing a number of companies within the high tech sector, Hansen pointed to Robert Spiegel, the author of *Net Strategy* (Dearborn, 2000) and *The Shoestring Entrepreneur's Guide to Internet Start-Ups* (St. Martin's Press, 2001), to support his position. Specifically Spiegel's assertion that the majority of companies that "failed did so not because they were bad ideas, but because they didn't solve anyone's problem."

While Spiegel concluded Hansen believed that "Many of the technology ideas were brilliant," it means very little at the end of the day "unless you can demonstrate a need that is getting met by these products, technology and ideas."

Over the years I have seen many careers take an unexpected turn toward the unemployment line. The reason was also fairly simple. The individuals, while experienced and talented, had lost sight of how their unique abilities were valued by the organizations for which they worked. In other words, they lost sight of how they solved their company's or client's problems and thus failed to make an indelible and enduring mark. In essence, they failed to build a legacy based on filling a tangible need.

The Legacy Factor

In the introduction to this book I talked about the importance of building a legacy. I discussed how the legacy that you leave behind is the imprint that lasts after you've retired or moved on. It is the enduring reflection of the impact that you've had on others throughout your career.

This being said, the steps you take to build your legacy also serve a pragmatic purpose in the here and now. Building a legacy brings greater meaning and purpose to what you do every day. When you see your professional career as more than a money-generating enterprise, you begin to grasp how you can make a difference among customers, colleagues, the community, and society at large. This brings far greater satisfaction than social standing or material possessions.

By this measure, how successful are you?

While you may enjoy financial rewards and a comfortable lifestyle—at least for the time being—are you achieving the maximum fulfillment from your life? This includes your effectiveness in terms of identifying the needs of those you seek to serve as well as how you are able to address those needs.

One Starfish at a Time

When you help others to succeed, you yourself cannot help but also reap and enjoy success.

So where do you begin in your efforts to serve the needs of others? After all, building a legacy is rarely accomplished with a single, overarching action or event. It is almost always the result of a series of small steps based on identifying and addressing a need.

Perhaps the fable of the old man and the starfish is a good place to start.

For those unfamiliar with the fable, one day an old man was walking along the beach and noticed that hundreds of starfish were being washed up on shore. Out of the water the starfish would soon die under the hot sun, so the old man began picking them up, one at a time, and throwing them back into the sea—a seemingly endless exercise that was repeated over and over and over again.

A little boy passing by stopped to ask the old man why he was throwing the starfish back into the sea, as it could not possibly make a difference since the waves were washing up as many as he threw back. The old man replied: "It may not make a difference overall, but to this one starfish in my hand it will make all the difference in the world."

Overall, the old man's actions demonstrated both integrity of purpose and a strong sense of service to others. While he could have gotten lost in the enormity of the number of starfish being washed up on shore, he wisely focused on doing only that of which he was capable. He didn't ignore the problem, deeming it to be a worthless cause, nor did he assume that someone else would step up to save the day. He instead looked to make a difference within the realms of his own values and capabilities.

Like the old man, you have to be proactive in seeking out ways to define and redefine your role and value proposition with your company and/or customers. In other words, you have to continually seek out the right fit! You have to find a need and position your unique ability or abilities to fill it.

Always Look for Ways to Earn Your Place in the World

Think back to when you were actively searching for your present job. Did you research the companies with whom you hoped to work? While far too many people make the mistake of looking for a job or position as opposed to seeking out the "right fit," you probably targeted those organizations for which you could provide a needed expertise.

In your efforts to select a company, did you seek to understand the challenges that you could address? Were you effective in explaining how you could deliver a solution based on your skills and value? Were you convinced that your expertise and ability could best serve the company's future vision? Were you confident that your boss would value your passion, respect your ambition, and become your sponsor for moving up?

The fact that you landed the job speaks to the effectiveness of your efforts. But this process should not stop once you have been with the same company for many years.

One of the key areas upon which this book has focused is on stepping out from behind the scenes and into the shared spotlight of organizational success on the front stage. Like the camera commercial in which the same individual actively seeks opportunities to be in everyone's picture, **you have to continuously seek ways to stay in the picture relative to your organization's changing needs.** You have to continually seek ways to find and maintain that perfect fit you originally had with your organization when you were first hired. You have to see your day-to-day work as earning your place in the world. You must also demonstrate your passion and enthusiasm daily so that others will feel your excitement.

Taking your cue once again from the old man and the starfish, this is a never-ending process of proving your value to your company and customers.

In this light, consider the following questions:

1. What difference have you made in the past? What difference are you making right now?
2. What key projects are you seeking out today that will result in greater value and importance to your organization's (or business's) future?

But what do you do if you can't find and fill an existing need? What if there are no starfish washing up on shore?

If You Can't Find a Need, Create One

Bearing in mind that companies are started by individuals, I recently posed the following question to my LinkedIn connections: What well-known company or companies do you believe best exemplify the phrase "Find a need and fill it"?

The responses I received were certainly varied and interesting, with names such as Virgin, Google, John Deere, and Apple popping up on more than one occasion.

However, one reader's response stood out by taking the question to a different yet complementary level when he made the assertion that, rather than finding a need to solve, Apple created one! The reader then went on to write:

There are two kinds of needs, one that is known as a problem and the other is something that is not consciously known but can be "created." Henry Ford's famous quote: "If I'd asked people what they want, they would have said a fast bullock cart." Same goes with Apple. No one thought about wanting a phone without many buttons on it. But when presented with one, they realized how simple their phones became by using an iPhone.

In creating a need, you will invariably position yourself as a trailblazer, and perhaps even a rainmaker.

Take Ross Perot, for example. While working for IBM, Perot recognized that his customers needed help processing their data and started EDS. He eventually sold EDS for 2.8 billion dollars.

Let's not overlook Make-up Art Cosmetics. Better known as M•A•C Cosmetics, the company was founded by Frank Toskan and Frank Angelo in 1984. While the product they developed in a kitchen was originally geared toward professionals in the beauty and fashion industry, its durability, ease of application, and inexpensive price tag ultimately took the consumer makeup market by storm. In 1998, M•A•C was acquired by Estée Lauder for an estimated 60 million dollars.

Then there is the story of the secretary at a small company. Mixing together flour with nail varnish, she used the concoction to white out her typing mistakes. As others noticed how well her inventive formula worked, she began receiving requests for "her product." Eventually, Bette Nesmith Graham sold the company she founded—Liquid Paper—to Gillette for 47 million dollars.

Of course, improving on an existing idea also provides great opportunities for delivering value, as demonstrated by Clemmons Wilson. Seeing that society was as a whole becoming more mobile, Wilson recognized the need for hotels that could accommodate families, and started one of the most successful chains in the world . . . Holiday Inn.

The John Deere Story

I found it interesting that one of the names that came up as a "find a need and fill it" company to my LinkedIn question was John Deere.

Today Deere & Company is the world's largest producer of farm equipment. However, back in 1825 John Deere was a journeyman blacksmith whose careful workmanship and ingenuity garnered great recognition.

Recognizing a growing need for a new type of plow, Deere, through trial and error, built one that was uniquely designed to scour itself clean as it moved through the soil. By 1868, Deere & Company was producing 13,000 plows annually, in what was at the time the largest factory in the Western states.

Deere's commitment to quality and ingenuity as a blacksmith became a hallmark of his new plow business, which was exemplified by the words, "I will never put my name on a plow that does not have in it the best that is in me."

How about you? Does your work represent the best that is in you?

Another Word about a Personal Mission Statement

Throughout this entire book I have talked about the importance of having a personal mission statement as it relates to establishing a guide for your career and your life based upon your values—

values, I might add, that will enable you to respond to either an existing need, or one that you create.

With John Deere, his promise that "I will never put my name on a plow that does not have in it the best that is in me" reflects an important personal value that was influential yet separate from John Deere the company.

This is an important point to remember, because while not all of us will build a company that we ultimately sell for millions of dollars or that becomes a globally recognized brand employing thousands of people, within our sphere of influence it is no less important.

In this regard, I was recently watching a television show about the late Merlin Olsen. For those of you who are football fans, you will undoubtedly remember Olsen as part of the daunting Los Angeles Rams' formidable defensive line that included Deacon Jones and Rosie Greer. Everyone else will likely remember Olsen from his television roles on the hit series *Little House on the Prairie* and *Father Murphy*.

What impressed me the most about Olsen was the fact that over the years he wrote a personal mission statement, which in 2010 was unveiled as part of a statue dedicated in his honor at his alma mater, Utah State University.

Here is what it reads:

> The focus of my life begins at home with family, loved ones and friends. I want to use my resources to create a secure environment that fosters love, learning, laughter and mutual success. I will protect and value integrity. I will admit and quickly correct my mistakes. I will be a self-starter. I will be a caring person. I will be a good listener with an open mind. I will continue to grow and learn. I will facilitate and celebrate the success of others.

I found it interesting that, even though his family and close friends were unaware that he had written a mission statement until it was discovered after his death on March 11, 2010, they were not surprised that he had one. Nor were they surprised at its content. This is because he lived his life according to these words each and every day.

During an interview, Olsen's brother commented that through his mission statement Merlin has set the bar high for his children. Regardless of what they choose to pursue as a career or life path, he stressed that the mission statement will always call upon them to give their very best.

Now *this* is a legacy in which the foundational elements can serve as a springboard, empowering you to proactively seek out ways that you can make a difference in the lives of others.

So what values does *your* personal mission statement reflect?

What needs does your personal mission statement enable you to identify and address?

Finally . . . Adopt an Attitude of Service

While you are working to answer a business need, remember to build your network as well as strive to be part of someone else's network. To do this, you should look for ways to apply your Unique Abilities in different situations. Perhaps you have a particular expertise or level of experience that would be valuable in a mentoring program at your company or in your industry.

In the meantime, if you have achieved success, be an inspiration to others. One way you can do this is by being a sounding board for someone else's ideas and dreams. Just be sure to listen with an open mind, and remember that you do not have to have all the answers, but your feedback may help someone to shape an action plan for the future.

> You do not have to try and save the world. Rather, make it your goal to improve your small corner of it.

By giving of yourself, you show people that they—and their dreams and goals—are worthwhile.

When you can put your career into this bigger context, you can find meaning in any job and in the process build your legacy.

Key Tips from This Chapter:

As the title for this chapter states, you must find a need and fill it! And if you can't find an existing need, then you have to create one.

The key point is that you must always be proactively looking for opportunities to be of value to your company and customers. Then and only then will you be able to build an enduring legacy that—like a Merlin Olsen—will define you in your lifetime, and long after you are gone.

Chapter 7—Gratitude, Power, and the Meaning of Life

"If the only prayer you said in your whole life was 'Thank you,' that would suffice."

—13th-century German philosopher Meister Eckhart

Gratitude is not a new concept for any of us. To this day, leadership books echo Eckhart's advice. In this chapter, I invite you to consider gratitude from three perspectives: a way to increase joy in good times; a way to lessen pain in bad times; and a way to build your brand by giving voice to the gratitude you naturally feel in your heart, because as novelist G. B. Stern said, "Silent gratitude isn't much use to anyone."

Be Grateful in Good Times

Thankfulness is a great equalizer. In good times, it leads us to acknowledge that our success does not belong to us alone. See your success and good fortune in the context of the support, love, and encouragement you have received over the years. Gratitude does not take away anything from you. Instead, I believe, it increases the joy you can gain from your success.

It is easy to see who understands the role of others in their success when listening to acceptance speeches at an awards dinner or watching the Academy Awards. Compare James Cameron's declaration that he was "king of the world" when he received the Oscar for the movie Titanic with Jamie Foxx's eloquent and moving speech of gratitude when he won an Oscar for his performance as Ray Charles in Ray. Fox ended his with a tearful tribute to his grandmother. Both speeches are on YouTube and are worth the study in contrast.

Those who are genuine in their gratitude toward family, friends, and mentors move us when they speak. And in that moment, a connection is created. **Gratitude should always be expressed whenever we feel grateful for something someone else has done for us.**

As a leader, you will naturally build those connections when you open your heart and share the glory of your successes with your team. Acknowledge others publicly and privately. Let them know that you understand what they contributed to your success by specifically sharing how the other person's actions, behaviors, and attributes helped you. That type of genuine interaction can build unbreakable bonds.

Be Grateful in Difficult Times

Gratitude helps us maintain perspective when we are faced with adversity. In the face of losing a job, a promotion, or a contract, we can still be grateful for the family, friends, and loved ones who are part of our lives. In the face of personal loss due to illness, death, or another tragedy, we can be grateful for those around us to support us or a job that gives us structure and meaning during a difficult time.

Just as you have a professional network for business opportunity, you must also be part of a resiliency circle of close family and friends who are there for each other when things are good and when they are not so good.

Once on the other side of personal or professional tragedy, be sure to go back and thank those who stood by you on your darkest days. Personally, I have experienced enormous gratitude for the support I received for the loss of my husband and my mother. My gratitude extended beyond family and friends when so many customers reached out to comfort me.

Giving Voice to Gratitude

The act of being grateful should not be limited to your family, friends, and colleagues. It should extend beyond your immediate circle to include your customers, business acquaintances, and members of your community.

Expressing gratitude strengthens both interpersonal and community relationships. Making others feel appreciated and valued encourages them to share in our milestones and vice versa.

There are many ways to give voice to your gratitude. Before doing so, think about the person you are thanking. Is he a private person? Would he appreciate public praise? Would a nice lunch together be appreciated or awkward for him? Observe how they thank others, as that is likely how they would prefer to be thanked.

Think about some of the nicest, most meaningful "thank yous" you have received in your life. What made them memorable?

Without prescribing any one way to say thank you, here are some ideas to consider:

- *Make it personal.* As many of you know, I am a fan of the handwritten note. No matter how virtual the world becomes, there is something deeply personal about a note penned in one's own handwriting on personal stationery.

- *Choose your words.* Don't just dash off the first thing that comes to your head. Take some time to craft your words—whether spoken or written—in a way that will hold meaning for the recipient.
- *Pick up the phone.* Ah, the telephone—that semi-useless instrument on your desk beside your computer. Remember, it can be easier to impart sincerity and emotion with your voice than with a keyboard.
- *Get creative.* There are many online tools that can help you create personalized mementos from photos of a shared event, or create some other symbolic way to memorialize a victory or milestone.
- *Give a small gift.* It is important that any thank-you gifts be appropriate and larger in meaning than in actual dollar value. You don't want your recipient to mistake a token of your thanks with payment for services rendered. For example, a Starbucks card for a devoted coffee drinker along with a personal note might be a winning combination.
- *Give the gift of time.* Two friends of mine stopped exchanging gifts a few years ago and started spending a day together on their birthdays. It has evolved into a tradition they both cherish as a way to thank each other for another year of friendship and support.

On a personal note, my son Sean was recently diagnosed with lupus. For those of you who don't know, lupus is a terminal disease in which the body's own defenses are turned against themselves. As my son was sitting in front of me at a restaurant after the diagnosis, he made the following comment that epitomized true gratitude. "Mom," he said, "however long I have in this world, I am grateful that I have lived life to the fullest. I have no regrets. I love what I do and I will live each day that I am given as a gift."

Thankfully, and a mere few days following the diagnosis, Sean called to say that the lab results were false positive. I didn't know if I should laugh or cry, but I knew I had just been taught the true meaning of gratitude. Specifically, we should live our lives with gratitude, not with regrets, because today is what truly counts.

I believe that the term *carpe diem* should end with the following important addition . . . seize the day—with gratitude!

How Do You Define Power?

"Power is likely defined differently at each stage of life. Having survived cancer last year, power has a new meaning for me. I have the power to cast a bright light in the world, the power to help others, to bring a smile to someone without one, to achieve whatever it is I desire."

Not that long ago, and as part of my research for a series of articles I was writing on the meaning of power, the above response to a question that I had posted to my LinkedIn community resonated with me deeply.

Similar to my son's response when he was misdiagnosed, I was amazed at the heartfelt and reflective insight of this individual. Having come through what I can only imagine was a very trying period in her life, she too expressed gratitude in the form of using her experience to positively impact the lives of others. In this way, gratitude and power are indeed connected.

Nowhere was the connection between gratitude and power better demonstrated than it was with Baby Jessica.

On October 14, 1987, 18-month-old Jessica McClure Morales fell into a well in the family's backyard. Over the next 58 hours, rescuers worked tirelessly to free her from the 8-inch-wide well casing 22 feet below the ground. With the world watching, Jessica was eventually pulled from the well.

For many, the story may have ended there. However, as a result of the accident, Jessica endured a total of 15 surgeries in the years following the incident, to repair the injuries that she had sustained from both the fall and being trapped for more than two days underground.

Besides having her small toe and part of her right foot removed, she also bears a diagonal scar across her forehead. When she was asked about having plastic surgery, Jessica said that she passed because the scar "shows who I am and the fact that I am here and that I could not have been here."

This demonstrates true gratitude, in that Jessica never forgot how fortunate she was to have had so many people working to save her. It also exemplifies courage in that she emerged from a harrowing experience with a positive attitude and a real sense of who she is.

Within the context of the above examples, what is true power, and who really has it? Is it determined by financial wealth? How about position or fame? Maybe it's the ability to have an impact on someone's life?

While I have always viewed wealth and fame as being fleeting in nature, I see true power as the ability to affect or have an impact on someone's life.

Starting with ourselves and our own life's direction, we are all powerful, especially when you take into account our ability to affect those around us. We may not necessarily have the immediate breadth of impact of someone like an Oprah Winfrey or Richard Branson or the President of the United States in terms of the actual number of people our decisions affect. But to those with whom we come in contact on a regular basis, we are no less significant.

Think about the power you have with children, friends, or colleagues seeking out your advice or needing a shoulder to lean on. What about the strangers to whom you reach out with a helping hand? Power is not about controlling others, but it is all about the impact you have when you use your power to make a difference.

Do you remember Liberty Mutual's "a helping hand is contagious" commercials? As one person witnessed an act of kindness by another, they themselves became motivated to lend a helping hand in a kind of pass-it-on or pay-it-forward manner.

So who, besides yourself, do your actions affect? Who do you inspire to "pass it on"? What personal changes would enhance your ability to serve others and empower them to be successful?

These are interesting questions on many levels, especially from the standpoint of your personal brand. Or to put it another way, if your brand is the sum of every experience others have had with you, what would people say? Would you be seen as considerate and helpful? Can you be relied upon when the chips are down?

The fact is that no matter how much effort someone expends to build the image they want to portray, if they fall short in their practical day-to-day interactions with others, it is this disconnect that will ultimately stand out. Building relationships and connecting with people, while helping them continually perform better, is how you expand your power.

So tell me, do your actions align with your brand? If they don't, you and you alone have the power to change! And at the end of the day, this is all the power that you really need.

So What Is the Meaning of Life?

While it is normal for people to be concerned with the here and now, how much time do we really spend reflecting on the enduring mark we want to leave in the sands of time?

For example, in the Middle Ages, artisans left their mark to uniquely identify themselves as the creators of their work, a practice that interestingly enough is where the word *character* comes from.

Your character and mark or brand is one and the same. It is therefore worthy of consideration because it goes to the heart of your life's purpose or mission. Identifying and understanding your purpose is why you have written a personal mission statement.

A personal mission statement tells you a lot about yourself and your present beliefs and paths. A personal mission statement serves as the foundation for the brand you ultimately create and through which you present your authentic self to the world.

So now we have come full circle.

Starting on page xxv , when I answered the question **Will my branding strategy actually work?** by introducing the concept of writing a personal mission statement, this entire book has focused on providing you with the necessary tools to build an enduring personal brand. In the next and final chapter I will share with you the invaluable insights that I have received from some of the most interesting, powerful, and well-known people from the world of business and beyond.

As you read this last chapter, it is my belief that you will be able to equate what we have talked about throughout the book with the success that each of these individuals has achieved on all levels of their lives.

Key Tips from This Chapter:

1. Extend your gratitude beyond family, friends, and colleagues to include customers, acquaintances, and members of your community.
2. Gratitude does not have to be a tangible gift, but can simply be expressing a feeling from your heart.
3. True power is the ability to affect or have an impact on our own choices as well as impact others' choices.
4. Use your power to enhance your ability to serve others and empower them to be successful.
5. By understanding your purpose, you will be creating greater meaning in your life.

Chapter 8—Industry Experts Speak Up on Personal Branding

"You will know me by my . . ."

The original concept of personal branding was first introduced by Napoleon Hill in 1937 in his book *Think and Grow Rich.* However, it wasn't until the 1980s that bestselling business author Tom Peters popularized the idea that individuals and not just corporations have a unique brand that defines who we are and what we have to offer to the world.

For more than twenty years I have had the privilege of meeting and talking with some of the world's most notable branding experts, including business leaders and, yes, even the occasional iconoclast.

In this, the penultimate chapter of *The Future of You: Creating Your Enduring Brand,* I am delighted to be able to share with you their thoughts regarding the question, **How do you build an enduring personal brand?**

What is worth noting is the fact that who you are and the brand that you build touch so many different areas of your life as well as the lives of others. For example, Shep Hyken, *New York Times* bestselling author of the books *The Amazement Revolution and The Cult of the Customer*, maintains that there is an undeniable link between one's brand and customer satisfaction.

A personal brand is something that positions you as the "go-to" person for whatever you want to be known for. You can be the go-to person within a larger organization or in an industry. Yet before sharing any ideas, the most important thing to keep in mind is that you can't really create your personal brand. The customer, be it internal (someone you work with) or external (someone you do business with), determines what your brand is. Their perception is their reality.

There is a business concept known as "Owning Your Mile." The mile is a metaphor. It's not really a distance, although it can be. A retail store may want to own the customers within a mile (or two or ten…) around their store. Someone like me, a customer service expert, may want to own the topic. What do you want to be known for? Why should people do business or come to you? If someone says, "When you look up the word ____ in the dictionary, you see their picture next to the definition," that "word" is their personal brand.

Finally, there is one thing that most people don't do in building their personal brand. They don't focus and aren't consistent. This is what you want to be known for, so don't change it up every six months or a year. Figure it out and then stay laser focused. As for consistency, you just can't announce it and hope people get it. You have to remind people over and over. My personal brand is amazing customer service. I end every e-mail with "Always Be Amazing." I write articles every week about creating amazing service. I tweet everyday on the same topic. It's focused and it's consistent.

Of course personal branding often extends to include the application of one's name to various products. Donald Trump is one person who comes to mind, as his real estate properties, restaurants, and the myriad of products that he endorses bear his name. While I might agree with the assertion that Trump is the ultimate iconoclast, I have to tell you that there is someone who

I believe runs a very close second. I am talking about Michael Cowpland.

Even though the Cowpland name may not carry the same swagger as Trump, the companies that he built have had no less of an impact on our daily lives. As the co-founder of Mitel and the founder of Corel, which brought us breakthrough software solutions such as CorelDRAW, Michael did not make a distinction between a personal and corporate brand when he offered the following advice for this book:

> Here are a few thoughts regarding how one would go about creating an enduring brand:
>
> 1. Find a market niche where you have a unique edge.
> 2. Use customer feedback to improve the product and carve out a bigger niche.
> 3. Identify your key benefits and advertise them with 10% of your gross margin.
> 4. Keep the core of the company central but use global advertising and promotion.

Larry Winget, who is known the world over as "the pit bull of personal development," is a five-time *New York Times* and *Wall Street Journal* bestselling author. A notable presence on television, Larry offered his view on personal branding:

> Branding people talk about finding the essence of who you are, etc. That's not it! As the most recognizable brand in the self-help industry, I can tell you that branding is not about knowing who you are but about knowing who you aren't. It's about being clear about what you aren't willing to do, the client base your product is not right for, the segment of society you aren't going to be the answer for. Too many people try to be all things to all people. It will never work. You can't make everyone happy. To build an enduring,

recognizable brand you have to be willing to have raving enemies, not just raving fans.

Besides being the host of the popular radio show *BrandTalk*, Dr. John Tantillo, "The Marketing Doctor," is a frequent contributor to Fox News Opinion online and the author of the book *People Buy Brands, Not Companies*. When I asked Dr. John for his thoughts on building an enduring brand, here is what he had to say:

Brands Are Always About Your Customers!

Whether building a personality or corporate brand, the essential component is to satisfy a need for a given Target Market that will eventually become your customers. To underscore this point, it is important to remember that brand building has very little to do with the marketer (the Brand Holder) and everything to do with one's customers.

This is best illustrated when Duncan Hines introduced an instant cake mix product where one would only have to add water to bake one of those delicious DH cakes. The new product was unsuccessful. Why? Because when consumers were asked why they did not buy this state-of-the-art innovation, they responded: "When I bake a cake for my family I want to do more than just add water." This clearly showed the good folks at Duncan Hines that there was an additional need that was overlooked—the need to be more involved in the baking process when preparing baked items for the family.

Times change and today this might not be as much of an issue as it was in the 1970s when Duncan Hines introduced this unique product to the American market. And so, for a brand to remain competitive, marketers must continue to research what their customers really want through quantitative and qualitative research. It's simple: Know your customers and respond to their changing needs so that your brand will always be there for them. This is the basis for all successful brands—know your brand and your customer's needs even more. And if your customers change, adapt accordingly.

What is interesting about the Duncan Hines example is that during a recent segment of the Food Network's *Recipe to Riches* show, the Executive Chairman of Loblaw Companies, Galen Weston, favored a product because it allowed the individual preparing the meal to be part of the process while still providing the convenience to accommodate a busy schedule.

Similar to Kentucky Fried Chicken's move toward introducing a healthier menu in the 1990s, only to return to their deep-fried roots in 2007, Dr. John's key point is that you have to—without fail—understand the changing interests of those you seek to serve.

Within the corporate world, branding extends beyond a company or the products and services it sells. Personal branding is an integral part of career success that extends all the way up to the executive suite.

Anu Hans, who is Group CPO and Vice President Pharmaceuticals at a global pharmaceutical company, offered a personal perspective on how to build an enduring brand. Based on her extensive and diverse experiences spanning many countries and positions over her 23-year career, Anu stresses the importance of knowing one's core values.

> It is important to recognize that positions, responsibilities, and even cultural circumstances will change over the course of time. Therefore the key is to be true to oneself. In essence, if you know and have a true sense of what you value and for what you stand, even though situations can from time to time become challenging, the constancy of knowing who you are will enable you to adapt to those changes.

In sharing her perspective on building an enduring brand, Anu's ability to adapt while remaining true to her personal values explains why she has had a long and successful career.

The metric for measuring a great CEO is diverse in that it can be based on dozens of factors. For those who head up a public company, share price or performance immediately come to mind as being a critical point of consideration. Others place an equal emphasis on a CEO's ability to make certain that their company continues to thrive. Of course to achieve this level of performance, the best CEOs have a strategic vision, a meticulous plan, and the ability to hire and keep excellent management.

Based on the above, it would be reasonable to conclude that when one is in a position of leadership, their personal brand and their management style can indeed be one and the same.

Take AstraZeneca President and CEO Elaine Campbell as an example. When I talked with Elaine, she shared her thoughts on the importance of being direct with members of her team regarding where she wants to take the company.

> While it is critical to be open with your views and enthusiastically present your vision, over the years I have recognized with increasing importance the need to not just engage, but to put enough of myself out there to create a base for debate, and then request or draw out differing points of view from my team. To be too strong in my vision is to shut down their participation and ability to challenge or build. In essence, I want to facilitate their ownership of the vision-building process rather than following what they think is the way I see things. For some on the team this can be uncharted territory, but the results are always better for the business.

Elaine went on to add that in this establish-build-challenge approach she doesn't pull any punches relative to discussing the merits of an idea or position, and she expects that the team will come fully prepared and engaged. Her ability to incorporate honest feedback within an environment of mutual respect has established her brand as a tough but fair-minded results-oriented CEO. This is in my opinion the kind of brand that makes for a great CEO.

The reference to the importance of honesty in terms of communicating with others takes on an even greater dimension when it comes to how you align your authentic self with your outward-facing brand.

When I spoke with two-time Mr. Universe winner Nordine Zouareg recently, his simple but powerful observation that "how you live your life is how you live your brand" highlighted what I consider to be the linchpin for both personal as well as professional success.

Besides being the author of the book *Mind Over Body*, Zouareg, who is also a Celebrity Wellness Coach (whose many clients have included luminaries such as Oprah Winfrey, Charlie Sheen, and Secretary of State John Kerry), stressed the importance of being able to walk the talk. "In essence, if there is a 'disconnect' between the image that you want to portray and the way in which you live your life (and values), you will inevitably undermine your brand and with it your creditability." The consequences of this kind of inconsistency, as demonstrated by my references to both Whitney Houston and the Wall Street character portrayed by Charlie Sheen earlier in this book, can be catastrophic.

According to Nordine, "You can't fool people forever—including yourself. By [sic] being true to 'who you are' and for what you stand at all times provides you with a firm and certain foundation upon which to build enduring success."

The authenticity question was also touched on by a good friend of mine, William J. White, a professor of industrial engineering and management sciences at Northwestern University. When

I approached Bill about providing his take on how to build an enduring brand, he stressed the importance of "authentic alignment." The Tiger Woods story was one of the first examples Bill offered to illustrate his point. As you will recall, Woods's image became somewhat tarnished due to his marital difficulties. Ironically, and despite losing sponsors, Woods is still the most recognized brand in golf. However, Bill cautioned that "his enduring presence (or the reason for it) has likely shifted from one of admiration to one in which the current 'fan base' may actually be following him to see if and when another chink in his armor may appear."

This "watching for failure" mindset is hardly the ideal circumstances or conditions under which one would want to base their brand, let alone pursue their livelihood.

The moral of the story is quite simple . . . you can fool all of the people some of the time, and some of the people all of the time, but you can't fool all of the people all of the time. Eventually who you really are and what you really stand for will come out, so you had better make certain that your outward face aligns with your inside values.

Alignment isn't limited to the relationship between who you are and who you want people to see.

Oftentimes, misalignment with corporate or customer objectives can prove fatal to one's career and ongoing success.

Senior Vice President, Human Resources and Health, Safety and Environment for Capital Power Peter Arnold talked about the importance of "matching your personal brand with the brand of your business." According to Peter:

> We all have a personal brand whether we are consciously aware of it or not—if we aren't, the people we work with are certainly aware of it through our actions and behaviors. Your

business results, personality, and alignment to the corporate values are all fundamental to creating your personal brand. It has been my experience that those individuals who produce high results but do not demonstrate the appropriate behaviors do not survive in an organization over the long run. To have a successful career it would be ideal to find a company that matches your style—in other words match your brand to the business. This will allow you to be authentic as a person.

Nowhere was the truth of Peter's words better demonstrated than with the terminations of Microsoft's Steven Sinofsky and Apple's Scott Forstall. Despite generating huge profits for their investors, the humiliating end to their respective careers would seem to suggest that while success is important, it might ultimately take a back seat to one's ability to work with and be liked by others.

What I also found most interesting about Peter's insights is that the ongoing alignment between individuals and the companies for whom they work is also a responsibility of the organization itself, and more specifically the present-day leadership. He emphasized this shared alignment responsibility when he stressed that "from an organizational standpoint, having a defined leadership brand will assist a company in recruiting and developing leaders who have significant impact on the culture of the company."

Section IV—End Results

The Brand Building Strategy

Chapter 9—Become Your Future!

Back at the beginning of the book we discussed measuring your results. More specifically, how do you create a metric by which you will be able to quantify your tangible success?

Similar to planning a trip, you have to first decide on where you want to go before you determine the route you will take to arrive at your intended destination. Of course, when it comes to building your brand, many believe that you have to first establish your goals before you can develop a clear-cut strategy or plan of action. I do not ascribe to this belief . . . at least not within the framework of the traditional order of things.

This is what makes *The Future of You* such a unique book.

I believe that in going through the process associated with my Brand Building Strategy the goals by which you would measure your success will have likely changed. The reason is that when you embark on a journey of what I will call brand self-discovery, you will inevitably challenge yourself in ways you probably never imagined. Starting with your values and the desire to be true to your authentic self, you will break the "old you" mold along with the inherent limitations that have defined who you think you are up to this point in time. You will then be free to see yourself and the world around you in an entirely new light of rediscovered enthusiasm and unlimited possibilities. And this, of course, is the ideal starting point from which to identify new goals that reflect a better understanding of who you are. With this new understanding, you will then be able to establish the true markers by which you will judge your success.

Nothing Succeeds like Success . . . and Perseverance!

By whatever measurement you define your success, be it a raise or promotion, successfully opening up a new business or being able to make a good living so that you can spend quality time with your family, one thing is certain . . . perseverance is the key to your achieving your goals.

Let's look at Danica Patrick.

Even though she placed 8th in the 55th running of the Daytona 500, Danica Patrick made history.

Besides having an opportunity to win the race right up until the very last lap, Patrick was already a big winner in that she became the first woman to win the pole position for the most important and prestigious race on the NASCAR calendar.

The benefits of her success extend well beyond the immediate fame that accompanies such a notable accomplishment. For example, according to the *Forbes* article "Danica Patrick Merchandise Flying Off Shelves Since Winning Daytona 500 Pole" by Kurt Badenhausen (Feb. 24, 2013), sales of licensed merchandise bearing Patrick's name are up . . . way up. I am talking about a 350 percent increase compared to the prior year's week before the Daytona 500, which was her "first appearance in the Great American Race!"

So what can we take away from Danica Patrick's performance?

Well to start, nothing succeeds like success! However, to be successful you have to have a plan and then work at achieving it. Throughout this book we have collaborated on creating your plan.

Like Patrick, who didn't just show up at the Daytona 500 this year for the first time and win the pole position, it is now time to put your plan into action.

When it comes to success, you have to work the plan without fear and without fail.

For Patrick, who began driving go-karts at the age of 10, this meant moving to Milton Keynes in England to advance her racing career when she turned 16. During her time on the British national series circuit, she came up against stiff competition, including future Formula 1 champion Jenson Button.

I can only imagine what it was like to be young, in a new country, going up against what would become some of the future greats in the racing world. But persevere she did, eventually returning to the US to become a consistent podium finisher in 2003, and ultimately being named Rookie of the Year in 2005 for both the Indianapolis 500 and the IndyCar 2005 Series season.

Of course the road to the 2013 Daytona 500 spotlight wasn't an easy drive. From the inevitable setbacks and the loss of her teammate Paul Dana, who was killed in a crash during a practice run for the Toyota Indy 300, to a variety of other challenges, Patrick persevered. She had a plan and a commitment to pursuing that plan.

Within this context you have to ask yourself the question . . . "What am I prepared to do to realize my goals?"

Within this answer is hidden in plain sight the road to your success, and like Danica Patrick, your ability to claim your pole position in the race to realize your dreams.

Cited References

Ellison, Ralph. *Invisible Man* (1952)

Emen, Jake. *Vince Lombardi: A Case Study in the Art of Leadership* (2007)

Fenchuk, Gary W. *Timeless Wisdom: A Treasury of Universal Truths* (2000)

Griffin, Michael. *Open-Door Policy, Closed-Lip Reality* (2012)

Haigh, David. *Brand Finance Annual Report* (2011)

Hill, Napoleon. *Think and Grow Rich* (2009)

Hoffman, Reid and Casnocha, Ben. *The Start-up of You: Adapt to the Future, Invest in Yourself, and Transform Your Career* (2012)

Lambert, Stephen. *Undercover Boss,* Episode 1, CBS Television (2009)

Nomura, Catherine and Waller, Julie. *Unique Ability: Creating the Life You Want* (2009)

Riborg Mann, Charles and Ransom Twiss, George. *Physics* (1910)

Spiegel, Robert. *Net Strategy* (2000) and *The Shoestring Entrepreneur's Guide to Internet Start-Ups* (2001)

Stone, Oliver and Weiser, Stanley. *Wall Street* (1987)

Thornton, Paul B., *The Answers Are on the Office Wall* (1994)

Usheroff, Roz. *Customize Your Career* (2004)

Van Doren Stern, Philip: *The Greatest Gift* (Movie: *It's A Wonderful Life*) (1939)